PENGUIN
JUGGLING WI

Neil Kelly joined advertising to see t
worked in four continents, culminat
1992 to 1994. *Juggling With Tigers* is h
a screenplay about corruption in the

He currently lives in San Francisco where he is completing a humorous book about being an alien. He's English, visiting Planet America.

Neil Kelly

Juggling With Tigers

Illustrations by Arul Raj

PENGUIN BOOKS

Penguin Books India (P) Ltd, 11 Community Centre, Panchsheel Park, New Delhi-110017, India
Penguin Books Ltd., 27 Wrights Lane, London W8 5TZ, UK
Penguin Books USA Inc., 375 Hudson Street, New York, NY 10014, USA
Penguin Books Australia Ltd., Ringwood, Victoria, Australia
Penguin Books Canada Ltd., 10 Alcorn Avenue, Suite 300, Toronto, Ontario M4V 3B2, Canada
Penguin Books (NZ) Ltd., 182-190 Wairau Road, Auckland 10, New Zealand

First published by Penguin Books India (P) Ltd. 1995

10 9 8 7 6 5 4 3 2

Typeset in Palatino by Digital Technologies and Printing Solutions, New Delhi

Contents

Namaste

In 1969 a friend was passing through Calcutta on his way overland to Europe. It was the heart of summer, hot and unbearably humid. The smallest effort brought out a sweat. Tempers were short but a long way away, 230,000 miles away, history was about to be made. At around 8.30 in the morning, local time, 21 July, Neil Armstrong became the first man to step on the moon. Being a fellow American my friend strained to hear those now famous words on a crackling transistor radio: 'One small step for man . . .'

'Isn't this great news? A man walking on the moon?' my friend enthused to an Indian standing next to him.

'No,' the latter flatly replied. 'It is not my moon.'

This book is about 'my India'. It's a chronicle of my attempts to do business and live in what was once described to me as the largest ungovernable democracy in the world. Since I was based in Delhi much of what follows focuses on the capital. Of course, Delhi is not India any more than London is England or New York's the United States, but it remains a strong microcosm and represents, for good and bad, much that is metropolitan India.

Because I'm an expatriate, 'my India' is by definition a foreigner's point of view; though I have talked to many Indians, both friends and strangers, travelled widely and tried to use domestic research, articles and statistics whenever and wherever possible. I have also tried to avoid some of the clichés and preconceptions that outsiders frequently bring with their baggage. Most foreigners have always arrogantly maintained that India is not an easy place to live in or visit. They argue the climate is unsympathetic, sickness is a constant threat, transportation and communications are dismal and the poor are a daily depressant. Under the Raj Britons died young or vanished into a gin bottle while today embassies and multinational companies consider

India to be a hardship posting and reward their staff with substantial bonuses and the promise of a softer assignment next time round.

I had been in India less than twenty-four hours when I was told a story about how over three quarters of the wives in one particular embassy spend the two or three years of their posting voluntarily imprisoned in their compound and living out of their commissary. The only time they ventured into the real world was to go to the airport. During the same conversation I was also told about the wife of an embassy psychiatrist. One morning she completely lost control, drove wildly off in her husband's car and then proceeded to scream hysterically out of the window: 'I'm going to kill you all!'

It's true, for some people India does prove too much. They let the frustrations trump the fascinations and leave in a mental strait-jacket. But even the most ardent fan will admit that the country frequently goes out of its way to make things difficult or just plain impossible. Complicating something simple is a way of life. Turning any task into a challenge is almost a philosophy and Indians suffer the consequences as much as foreigners. They may know the ropes and some of the tricks those ropes can perform but it doesn't make coping any the easier. For in India, nothing is quite what it seems.

*

The world of advertising is not quite what is seems, either. From the outside it often appears to be a glamorous, frivolous even self-indulgent profession, selling stereotypical dreams to avaricious and gullible consumers. From the inside, where I have been for some twenty years, I can report that few of us actually know how to sell. Instead we work on a hunch and veil it under a cloak of research, persuasion and jargon. The emperor's new clothes. In fact, most advertisements confirm rather than manipulate the buyer's freedom of choice. As for the glamorous side of the business—well, judge for yourself once you've finished this book.

For me, advertising has always seemed to be a great way of seeing the world. Being a copywriter it was a case of 'have pen will travel.' In London, where I began, I would continually write scripts that required me to travel to the far corners of the earth in order to pay homage to a chocolate bar or a bottle of shampoo. Sadly, I was only allowed to follow my pen on a couple of occasions. I therefore eventually decided that if the mountains would not come to me, I would go to the mountains.

My first overseas posting was to Gothenburg, in Sweden, where I was hired to be the international creative director of an agency that had no international business. But it did have a massive tax bill; Sweden, then, being one of the world's most highly taxed nations. My job, as far as I could ascertain, was to be a 'tax loss'. I was given a new Volvo, a luxury apartment by the waterside, a liberal expense account and, since it was summer, told to take a month's vacation. One month became two and then I was sent to New York for reasons never fully explained. While there my immediate boss revealed that on returning he intended to resign and start Sweden's first communist advertising agency. He already had one account for Tor Lines, a ferry company serving three ports, all of which had an association with Karl Marx. Would I like to join him? I reluctantly declined and a few days later I was summoned to Stockholm to meet the chairman. He told me that the agency was now losing so much money they would have to lose me. I was no longer a tax deductible item.

My next trip abroad took me briefly, but not briefly enough, to Lagos—possibly the world's worst city. My client sold trucks there and wanted to sell more. He thought he understood the market by selling them sans doors so more air could circulate through the cab, but he was being outsold by his rivals who equipped their trucks with doors. I found out why. The doors of the competition's trucks were removed by the drivers who then sold them as walls for slum housing, complete with roll down windows.

In another African country, Egypt, I came across the longest billboard in the world. It was for Schweppes, and the government had paid for its erection and maintenance in order to hide the poor from the eyes of those driving to and from the airport. The company I worked for in Cairo had been started by a rock musician who had moved on to writing jingles, directing commercials and finally running the city's largest agency. He warned me shortly after I arrived that doing business was difficult because there was no telephone directory and the phone company kept changing customers' numbers without revealing what the new ones were. In a sense this was an extreme rehearsal for what lay ahead in India.

It was while working in Hong Kong that I received my first Indian premonition. In the middle of a presentation for a pizza account I was called from the boardroom. The receptionist said there was a man waiting who insisted it was 'absolutely imperative' he saw me. As I walked in to the reception a plump and swarthy Indian stood up and loudly declared: 'You have the eyes of Christ!' He turned out to be a roaming swami who maintained he'd been directed to find me to reveal that I would die in '88. This was 1987. 'In 'eighty-eigtht or when I'm eighty-eight?' I anxiously enquired. It was a big difference. 'I cannot say,' he replied, although had I crossed his palm with a substantial dollar note I'm sure the matter would have become clarified.

Anyway, I'm still alive. Just.

It was to be another five years before I came to live in his homeland during which my pen and I spent time in Japan, China, Korea, Taiwan, Malaysia, the Philippines, Indonesia, Australia, New Zealand and finally Atlanta, Georgia; a futuristic if sterile city blessed with the next Olympic Games and cursed with the kind of accent chewing gum would have if it could speak.

*

Before I came to live in India, I came to visit; a quick suck-it-and-see inspection that involved spending twenty hours in Bombay and not much longer in Delhi. The jet lag outlasted my stay and as a consequence I ended up agreeing to a bunch of vague terms committing me to at least two years of subcontinental employment. Not many people grant their own arrest warrant, nor do many foreigners go and work for an Indian advertising agency. While I was there I was the only European doing so.

During that all too brief encounter I had failed to fully comprehend what I might be letting myself in for—least of all the heat, since I had travelled in February. To be fair the creative director I was replacing gave me a candid warning. 'You won't last a month if you come,' he said. 'You don't understand India.

Advertising here is done differently.' He was wrong on the first point. I lasted two years. But he was correct on the second. Advertising in India is done differently, as is almost every other human activity. In a further attempt to dissuade me he then took me out for a five-hour liquid lunch followed almost immediately by a six-hour liquid dinner. When I tried to drunkenly extricate myself and take a taxi to the airport he insisted on coming with me, oscillating wildly between intoxicated giggles and melancholic tears. Managing somehow to get through security he pursued me to the lounge. 'Don't come back,' he pleaded as my flight was called. 'You'll regret it.'

Five months later I came back but I didn't regret it. Well, only occasionally as my health or sanity threatened to disappear. Having lived or worked in almost every Asian country India has provided me with the ultimate experience; a Wonderland beyond even Lewis Carroll's lucid imagination which succeeded in bombarding my every sense, in every sense. I could not have written this book about any lesser land nor, I suspect, about any other profession.

Spending too long in a hot climate can make the memory melt. Fortunately, during my stay I kept a diary. Mae West once remarked: 'Keep a diary and one day it will keep you.' As I leave India for pastures new I appreciate her advice. I also appreciate the help given to me by colleagues, clients, friends and passing acquaintances who provided the incidents on which the following stories are based.

The Indian Rope Trick

Delhi in the summer is incineratingly hot. So hot that roads melt, vegetables come out of the soil already cooked and humans come close to spontaneous combustion, especially newcomers. Look at any temperature chart and Delhi is the hottest city on earth for a good part of the year. The British, never naturally at home with the heat, must have been as mad as dogs in deciding to make it their imperial capital in 1911, moving from Calcutta which was almost as climatically unbearable. A case of out of the frying pan, into the fire. Eventually, realizing their grand mistake, they would move the machinery of government, along with all its operators and spare parts, to the more clement hill station of Simla and there, with gins and Pimms, wait until the temperatures subsided.

It was July the Fourth the morning I arrived. Independence Day in the States, Inflammation Day in Delhi. The temperature outside the airport was 45 degrees Celsius, around 113 Fahrenheit. When body temperature is exceeded by that many external degrees some thermodynamic law must come into play causing, or so I felt, the molecules to randomly expand and shift. Within seconds I was transformed from a jet-setting, advertising executive into a semi-liquid, subatomic mass. And if my very being had changed its appearance so, it seemed, had my name. As I scanned the row of cards held hopefully high—MR SMITH, BRITISH LEYLAND; HERE SCHMIDT, BAYER—I came across a MR CHILLI with my company's name below. Unquestionably, I was hot enough to qualify.

The man holding the card was short and stubby with a huge, bushy moustache. He greeted me with the enthusiasm of a relative and almost as keenly took my trolley with its assortment of fifteen bags and cases. I asked him his name. He gave in reply one of the longest names in the world. It sounded like a complicated, polysyllabic patented medicine but said in reverse, or in Russian, or both. I enquired whether he spoke English.

'Yes, sir,' he snapped back like a soldier answering a general.

'Good. Well, um, please take me straight to the hotel.'

'Yes, sir.'

We walked over to what looked like an ancient Morris Oxford the colour of cream of chicken soup. It was called, rather pretentiously, an Ambassador. This was my first exposure to the contradictory nature of India. Such a name elsewhere would have been attached to a sleek luxury limousine with leather upholstery, walnut panelling and packed with sophisticated gadgets. But this particular vehicle looked more like a roly-poly toy car, lacking only a large key sticking out of the roof.

Um, as I had elected to call him, spent an age trying different permutations with my luggage as if they were parts of a giant leather puzzle. I waited for him to arrive at a solution with my hair feeling like it was about to ignite.

'It's very hot,' I said stating the obvious.

'Yes, sir,' he willingly agreed.

I climbed into his mobile oven and we set off. The car's ancient air-conditioning hopelessly attempted to battle with the heat but it proved to be marginally cooler with the windows wound down. For some thirty minutes we sweated our way across a nondescript landscape of half-built or half-ruined buildings, dusty fields and rickety billboards—one of which showed a giant, grinning devil who perversely welcomed newcomers to Delhi. With the car, and its passenger, on the point of dying from heat exhaustion we finally stopped outside a dilapidated tower block which looked like it had been transplanted from Beirut.

'This is my hotel?' I asked incredulously.

'Yes, sir.'

My molecular structure shifted uneasily again as a sense of insecure doom mingled with the heat and the jet-lag. 'No, this can't be right,' I almost pleaded. 'The building's derelict.'

'Yes, sir.'

'What's the name of this hotel?'

'Yes, sir.'

Then I realized: Um could speak English, two words of it. However, an even worse realization came a few minutes later when I discovered this ramshackle erection contained my new place of employment. During my fleeting visit in February I had never visited the office; thanks, mainly, to my malcontented predecessor monopolizing my time by trying to drown me in alcohol. Had I done so I might have had second thoughts. This was not Madison Avenue. Most of the communal windows had been smashed, graffiti and torn posters covered the walls and the open-fronted lift lobby reeked of rotting garbage. And yet, ironically, a large and stern warning promised a substantial fine for anyone found guilty of defacing the place—landlord excluded.

There were three lifts but only one was working. Stepping in I noticed its certificate of inspection was way out of date, both the emergency button and emergency light had disappeared and the floor buttons had been jumbled into a nonsensical order. Even the ceiling fan had vanished or been stolen. It was a metaphor but whether for my company, the country or my career I am still not sure.

I found the button for the thirteenth floor, the top floor, my new job, and the lift began its slow, creaking ascent. On the back wall there was a framed list of rules. Although the glass had been smashed it was still possible to read them. One of them stated: DO NOT FEEL PANICKY IF YOU ARE STRUCK. YOU ARE SAEF INSIDE. From that moment onwards I panicked whenever I stepped into the lift.

Panic, according to a locally produced handbook I came across, is apparently one of the first reactions foreigners experience on arriving in India. Euphemistically, and a shade patronizingly, it is often called culture shock and produces a number of physical and psychological symptoms such as stomach disorders, loss of appetite, sleep disturbances, compulsive drinking, depression, anxiety, moodiness, irritability and apathy. Working in advertising for so many years I had already picked up most of these ailments, so I felt reasonably at home.

The lift finally reached the summit and I nervously stepped out to be confronted with the sight of a crouched man violently hitting a piece of wood with a claw hammer. He looked up and smiled at me and then pointed towards the agency's reception, devoid of a receptionist. I could only assume the woodworker, or woodbasher, unconventionally played that role.

Another contradiction.

Advertising agencies around the world make a point of hiring glamorous bimbos to greet and, if all else fails, seduce clients. The smiling face of the company. This agency not only had no face, it barely had a body. The reception looked more like the hospitality lounge of some small and impoverished West African airline. Windowless, gloomy and threadbare. An ancient switchboard rang but no-one bothered to answer it. A few tattered advertisements hung limply on a stained cork board and this was the only clue that I had found the right office. I stood and waited, unsure of whether to answer the phone or use it to find out the time of the next plane leaving India.

'Hello, sir. I'm the office manager.'

I turned. The voice belonged to a young man, almost a boy, with a captivating grin and a shock of curly black hair.

'Good morning,' I said. In truth I no longer had any idea whether it was morning, afternoon or even if I was still in the twentieth century.

'I trust you had a pleasant flight,' he added.

In fact, it had been anything but pleasant. Over twenty hours, with a brief transit in London, I had sat next to a talkative and increasingly intoxicated Swede who came to India two or three times a year to blow the place up. His company provided explosives to tunnel and mine for minerals, primarily in Bihar—a state rich in natural resources but possessing some of the world's poorest people. At some point during the flight he had informed me that he was carrying an apocalyptic amount of explosives in the cargo hold beneath us. 'Purfffectly shafe,' he tried to drunkenly assure me. 'I haf the fhuses in my bwiefcase.'

'The flight was okay,' I lied. 'What's your name?'

'Krishnan,' he replied. 'I come from Kerala.'

'Really? That's a state in the South, isn't it?'

'Yes, sir. It has the highest literacy rate in India,' he proudly informed me. 'I can write and read English very well.'

'That's good to know.'

'But I keep it a secret,' he went on to cryptically add.

'Why?'

'Because I'm clever,' he replied even more cyptically.

Being on the top floor with the outside temperature hovering close to Mercury's this was, at least in one sense, a hot agency.

Antiquated fans fought against impossible odds to stop the staff from dissolving. Despite the heat most seemed cheerful and I was introduced to them one by one. Again, as with Um, I found it extremely difficult to pronounce most of their names let alone remember them. In total there were about forty-three. I say 'about' because on asking three different people how many worked for the company I was presented with three different numbers. Taking the average gave me the figure of forty-three.

'But not everyone works every day,' Krishnan told me.

'I don't understand. What do you mean not everyone works every day?'

He gently shook his head as he thought about something, presumably my question, for a few moments. 'Some people have to be sick.'

'Have to be? You mean it's obligatory?'

'I'm sorry?'

'Compulsory?' I tried.

'Many people are sick in India,' he said, retreating into a truism.

I was soon to realize that the staff not only took time off when they were sick, either by choice or by decree, they also took time off when someone else was sick, like a relative or even a friend. And their absence was not for just a day. Often it was for weeks.

'Vikki takes every Thursday off,' Krishnan added.

Vikki was my secretary; more precisely, the communal secretary and general dogsbody. Also from Kerala, this was the first secretary I'd ever had who wore a beard.

'Why Thursdays? Has it something to do with his religion?'

'No, no. That's the day he washes his clothes.'

'Why can't he wash his clothes in the evening or in the morning before he comes to work?' I suggested.

'He only has one set.'

He could only afford one set of clothes. Vikki was earning every month about half of what I was about to spend, or rather what my new company was about to spend, on my hotel room per night. However, Vikki didn't just take Thursdays off. Sometimes he took the whole month off, vanished down South to try and find an arranged wife. He always returned a confirmed bachelor and no one, except myself, found his part-time relationship with the company out of the ordinary. The logic, I guess, was that if some had to be sick, Vikki had to be married.

There was another reason why not everyone worked every day. Power cuts. I had been in the office less than an hour when the place was plunged into darkness. Without the fans the temperature quickly soared into tandoor mode.

'How long will we be without power?' I asked.

Krishnan shrugged. 'Sometimes one hour. Sometimes longer. Impossible to know. Best you go to hotel.'

'How many power cuts are there every day?' I continued to enquire.

'Five. Maybe six. During summer always bad.'

'Why don't we buy a generator?' I suggested.

'Yes, sir,' he agreed, but we never did.

Um was instructed to drive me to a hotel which was close, a shade too close to the agency. Being a senior executive I had selfishly expected to be cocooned in five-star luxury, but the only stars this hotel possessed could be seen out of the window after dusk. It was named after the prince who became Buddha, but I was in urgent need of hedonism rather than Buddhism. However, I reasoned that at least I could shower, get a few hours sleep and then, once fortified, take on the challenge of finding another, superior hotel. While a team of bell boys carried my fifteen bags and cases to an undetermined destination I asked the receptionist for a quiet room.

'Room 611 is very quiet room, sir,' he assured me handing over the key. 'Please enjoy your stay.'

I have always hated orange. Why any interior designer employs its use is beyond me. It's about as restful as an air-raid. Room 611 was almost entirely orange: walls , curtains and carpet. Even the bedspread. The only thing not orange was the water, because there wasn't any.

I picked up the orange phone and dialled the front desk. 'There's no water in my room,' I said.

'I am afraid at the moment we are having a water problem in that side of the building,' came the explanation.

'Then why did you give me a room in that side?'

'Because you wanted a quiet room, sir.'

What I wanted was for the S.A.S. to airlift me out. What I got

instead was a phone call. It was my Indian partner.

'Good morning, Neil. Welcome to India. I hope you had a pleasant flight,' he purred.

Whether or not newcomers had a pleasant flight was obviously of critical importance to my new agency. Since he had paid for it I mumbled a semi-affirmative reply and went on to remark, as politely as I could, how the hotel was less than acceptable.

'Really?' He sounded surprised, almost upset. 'We chose it because it's close to the office.'

'To be honest I'd rather put comfort over convenience.'

'Whatever you wish. May I suggest you move to the—.' He mentioned an international chain. 'They used to be our client. I'll get someone to make a reservation. You'll find the car waiting downstairs. Have a rest and we'll meet for dinner.'

'I'm checking out,' I told the receptionist a few minutes later.

'But you've just checked in, sir.'

'Call me eccentric. Can you please have someone collect the bags from my room?'

Um was stretched out on the back seat fast asleep. He looked startled on being woken up, unsure of where he was or who I was. He glanced at his watch as if to check he hadn't been sleeping for hours.

'New hotel,' I told him and mentioned its name very slowly.

'Yes, sir,' he said as the mystified team of bell boys began loading the car.

'Do you understand?' I didn't want to end up at a hospital instead of a hotel. Then again, perhaps I did.

He smiled back at me like a patient father. 'Yes, sir,' he repeated.

Our trip to the second hotel showed me the imperial side of the capital, the elegant web designed by Lutyens. The wide, tree-lined roads with their roomy, classical, white bungalows seemed at odds—contradicted—the congested, honking, smoking trucks, buses and auto-rickshaws. Even more incongruous were the sacred but emaciated nomadic cows grazing in the fast lane. Scooters and 'mobikes' carried entire families; mum, dad and child squeezed on to the seat with baby resting on the handlebars, like an amateur circus act. Push bikes wobbled among and against the traffic, supporting two, often three people. Buses conveyed hundreds: corroded tins of baked humans with arms poking out of the windows to indicate every turn.

I had been in the car about twenty minutes, windows wound down, soaking up the atmosphere, when I started coughing. Little did I know then that Delhi had become one of the most polluted cities in the world, to the point where respiratory diseases were twelve times the national average. As a result one in three of its residents has some kind of complaint. A few days after my arrival I read a report by the former chief executive of the city council who apocalyptically declared: 'By the year 2000 Delhi will be an atmospheric gas chamber.'

Take a deep breath and say AARGH!

No wonder I was coughing like a consumptive by the time I checked into my next hotel. And I continued coughing as I lay on the bed in my executive floor room trying to sleep. A Delhi frog, possibly an iguana, had moved into my throat and refused to be evicted. At six, feeling like I hadn't slept for a week, I coughed my way to the bar. It was time for a dose of colonial medicine. I ordered a gin and tonic.

'Large or small, sir?' the waiter asked.

'Large, please.'

'Domestic or imported?'

'Domestic.'

'With or without lemon?'

'Whatever.' I felt I was unwillingly taking part in a quiz show. The drink arrived and I gratefully downed it in seconds. Calling the waiter back I asked for another.

'Another?' He looked bewildered. 'Sir, was there something wrong with the first one?'

There was a German tourist sitting at the table next to me. My encounter with the waiter had clearly amused him. 'You on a tour, too?' he asked.

'No, I've come here to live,' I replied.

He blinked back at me and then announced: '*Nein.* Not possible.'

I assured him it was and that nearly a billion had also made India their home; although, admittedly, not all of them by choice.

He shook his head. 'I could never live here. It is a crazy

country.' He made the word 'crazy' seem to last forever.

'Crazy in what sense?'

He looked around then pulled his chair closer. 'I speak English good, no?' he said. 'But people here speak a different English. *Ja*. *Ja*. I think so.'

'Different in terms of accent?'

'*Nein*. Accents I can understand. I have an accent, yes?' He took a swig of his beer. 'English spoken here is different, I think so, because they don't always know that the words mean.'

*

My Indian partner was very tall and very thin, almost two dimensional. When he was eighteen he had gone to university in Chicago. It was his first visit to the States. On arriving there he had been astonished on walking into a Burger King to find a WHOPPER on sale. Where he came from it meant a male member. Since he was a vegetarian he spent his time in the Windy City living on an exclusive diet of french fries and milk shakes; a notoriously windy combination. After eight years he was summoned back to Bombay by his father to help rebuild the family's advertising agency. He became a superb adman, persuasive and confident. Sometimes, however, he had difficulty making up his mind. For him decisions had no 'to be taken by' stamped on them. They possessed an eternal shelf life. Then, out of the blue and completely out of character, he made an almighty decision. He offered me a job.

By the time he joined me at the bar I had drowned four or five disputably wrong gin and tonics, but if I was starting to feel better inside I obviously still had a few problems outside.

'Gosh! What's wrong with you?' he enquired gingerly shaking my hand. From the alarmed look on his face he must have thought he had hired a potential cadaver.

'No sleep for about two days and a severe case of asphyxiation could be part of the problem,' I said between coughs.

'You didn't take a nap this afternoon?'

'Every time I fell asleep I coughed myself awake.'

'Takes some adjustment, India. You'll soon get the hang of it,' he promised.

Over an Italian dinner with Californian wine we discussed in

English the state of the agency. It was similarly mixed-up. The managing director, who had been out during my brief morning visit, had threatened to get out for good. The creative director I had replaced was still coming to work after hours in order to upset or poach my staff. Morale was at an all time low. The few clients we still possessed were growing increasingly unhappy and the whole operation was making a hefty loss.

'Things can only get better,' my partner sheepishly grinned. He didn't sound too confident.

The situation, unfortunately, was not new to me. In 1985, I had flown out to Hong Kong to work for an agency that was in a similar state of disarray. The managing director had also resigned taking most of the staff and accounts with him. He left behind a junior accountant, a senior Chinese copywriter and the tea lady. Initially, the three accounts that remained sounded reasonable: a soup, a bank and a cigarette account, but when back translated into English from their Cantonese names they lost much of their appeal. The soup was called 'Clear Shit', the bank was known as the 'Bank of Ghouls' and West cigarettes became 'Death' cigarettes.

In lieu of dessert my partner began drawing an organizational chart on the back of his napkin. It was supposed to show how the 'new, improved' agency would operate and how it would relate to the other five agencies within the Indian network. When he had finished it looked like a ball of steel wool.

'It looks very complicated,' I remarked.

He turned it round, looked at it from a different perspective. 'Maybe needs refining a little, but the principle's fine.'

Later, back in bed, body clock overwound, I flicked through a copy of the TIMES OF INDIA. One story caught my disorientated attention. A drunken elephant had gone on the rampage and killed several villagers in Bihar. How, I tried to imagine as sleep finally accepted me, could an elephant get drunk?

*

The explosive Swede, my too intimate companion on the long flight to India, had told me there were three ways of doing business in the subcontinent; the right way, the wrong way and the Indian way. On arriving at work the next morning I discovered there was actually a fourth way: my agency's way.

'Morning, Mr Killy,' I was welcomed by an account director sitting behind my desk who had been urgently scribbling something on a pad as I walked in.

'Kelly. The name's Kelly,' I gently corrected him.

'Kelly Killy?'

'Just Kelly. Neil Kelly. Call me Neil,' I suggested.

Account directors are supposed to run a client's business. I had been discreetly informed the night before, however, that this particular one might have a problem running a bath.

'Ah yes, Kneeel,' he said turning my name into an extended verb. 'Would you like to have a meeting?'

'What, now?'

'Now, no.' He let out a nervous giggle. 'Later this morning. With a client.'

'Which client?'

'He manufactures audio cassettes. Now he wants to sell televisions.' He paused. 'I must be frank and admit that lately he has been giving me a big headache.'

'Why's that?'

'He has not paid any of our invoices for almost a year.' he replied. 'Worse, now he is threatening to fire us.'

'Why does he want to fire us?'

'He thinks we are too expensive.'

I was confused. 'But you just said he's never paid us.'

'Correct. That is why he hasn't paid us, because he thinks we're too expensive.'

I came to call this kind of tautological exchange the Indian Rope Trick because it ties rational thought into knots and strings at least one of the parties along until they're left hanging in thin air.

We left in Um's chicken soup Ambassador and headed north. The client was located in Old Delhi but neither Um nor the account director seemed to know precisely where. Whereas New Delhi conformed to a neat geometrical pattern, Old Delhi was like driving into a huge vat of spaghetti; a spicy dish of twisting, narrow lanes barely wider than our car and sometimes not even as wide. Into this Bolognese had been poured pedal rickshaws, auto-rickshaws, scooters, taxis, carts, cattle, goats and a rich assortment of busy people. As we became ever more entangled, frequently stopping to ask for directions, I couldn't contain myself.

'What is so funny, Kneeel?' the account director nervously asked.

'I knew we might have problems finding new clients,' I replied, 'but I didn't know it would be so hard finding existing ones.'

The account director chuckled. Um, however, roared. Did he, perhaps, understand English fluently? A driver in disguise?

'What time did you set the meeting for?' I asked, managing to supress my levity.

'Eleven o'clock.'

'We're very late.' I said. It was almost twelve.

'In India everyone is late. It is not a problem,' I was assured.

I had just passed through another subcontinental rite.

In India time often appears to be on valium. Like the Hindu notion of Anadi (Creation) it has no beginning and no end. In fact, such is the general apathy towards the passing of time that there are no words in Hindi for early or late and there is only one word, the same word, for yesterday and tomorrow. India is a vast hour-glass full of shifting people who care little about precise, chronological measurements like seconds and minutes. Despite its width—over two thousand miles—India has only one time zone and even that is half an hour out of sync with the world's other time zones.

We finally reached the client's office, disturbingly run down and squeezed into the end of a dark lane, close to one o' clock. My colleague's assurance that being late would not present a problem proved a fallacy because those we were supposed to meet had gone for lunch. We waited in a tiny room with no air-conditioning until they returned. The average sauna would have been larger and marginally less hot.

'Can I use the toilet?' I eventually had to ask.

A peon escorted me down a dingy corridor lined with large cardboard boxes. 'It is very dirty,' he proudly announced as he pushed the door open. It was. The Black Hole of Delhi. SAVE WATER someone had crudely written on the wall but there was no sign of a tap. By the time I returned to the conference sauna four men from the client side had arrived and taken the only available seats. I was forced to stand.

'This is Mr Kneeel Kelly, our new creative guru from the United States of America. He's an Englishman,' the account director grandly, if paradoxically, announced. He then appeared to fall asleep.

'So, Mr Keddy, what's the big idea?'

'I'm sorry?' I didn't even have an idea who was asking the question since my colleague had failed to introduce us.

'The big idea that will make our televisions sell like hot cakes,' the mystery man elaborated.

'I don't know. Not yet. I thought we were here to pick up a brief? I need to know more about your business.'

A bout of hectic Hindi followed for which the account director came briefly out of his doze. Finally the question master reverted to English. 'We need advertisements in the paper by this weekend. No time to waste. Please give us one of your clever ideas that has worked splendidly before.'

I was nonplussed. 'That's not the way I, we work. We always try to give our clients an idea which uniquely matches their marketing needs.'

Good text book stuff but wasted here. Their need was for an original idea that had worked before. That was all they wanted and I suspected they wanted it before I left. My suspicions were confirmed when I was handed a pen and a sheet of paper.

For a moment I was tempted to give them an old concept to get away from the confined heat. The egocentric Egyptian I had briefly worked for in Cairo would have done just that in a similar situation. He believed an idea could be hawked around until a client bought it. He had one which involved a red Indian. He tried it first on Kodak. The Indian, in full ceremonial dress, walked into a processing centre and said, 'How!' The man behind the counter produced an envelope of developed photographs and said, 'Now!' To which the impressed Indian exclaimed, 'Wow!' When Kodak declined this creative gem he offered it to Kentucky Fried Chicken, changing the setting to a restaurant and transforming the envelope into a chicken leg. They, too, didn't say 'Wow!' to the concept and as I was returning to England he was about to present it to Egypt Air, with the leg of chicken becoming an air ticket.

'Look, you need to tell me more about the product,' I said back in the Old Delhi sauna.

'It's a television,' someone helpfully chipped in.

'Yes, I know, but what makes it special?'

'Nothing.'

'It's cheaper,' another offered.

'No it's not,' his colleague disagreed.

'Can't we say it gives you better programmes?' a previously silent sage suggested.

WHAT? Who was this man? 'All tvs show the same programmes,' I almost shouted.

'Technically, I agree, but surely we can promise more. Isn't that the role of advertising?'

There is an unwritten law in advertising that clients always believe their products are better than they actually are; a sort of proud father and reluctant son relationship. I met one client in Singapore who wanted to say his toothbrushes were recommended by nine dentists out of ten. When I asked him if he could substantiate this claim he appeared doubtful. He suggested instead that I say 'Denis', muffled and quickly, in the commercial. 'Nine out of ten Denis's prefer . . . Everyone will think we're saying "Dentists",' he tried unsuccessfully to convince me.

'I'll promise one thing,' I said to the Delhi merchant of hyperbole. 'I'll get back with a campaign tomorrow. I need a few hours alone.' I urgently needed to wallow in a bath of ice.

'Did you enjoy that?' asked the account director as Um negotiated our escape out of the labyrinth. He spoke like we had just been to see a movie together.

'No, not much. It was, I feel, a case of too many Indians and not enough chiefs,' I replied not intentionally trying to be witty. 'Also, I wish you'd warned me they were expecting to see some work.'

'You didn't read the note I left you?' he said raising an eyebrow. So that's what he had been scribbling when I entered my office. I had never bothered to check.

'No. Why? What did it say?'

'Please produce advertisement to sell television.'

'Gee! That's not much of a brief, is it? Anyway, even if I had read it I couldn't have helped. We had the meeting about an hour later.' We stopped at a traffic light and a beggar, seeing a European, ran to my side of the car. She looked heavily pregnant. Um waved her away and as she left I saw her nonchalantly remove a pillow from under her blouse, walk to the side of the road and squat down on it. For a moment I lost my train of thought. 'Why didn't you brief it out a week ago?' I eventually resumed.

'You weren't here a week ago.'

I could tell the Indian Rope was on the verge of unreeling like a fishing line hooked into a record-breaking marlin. I decided to cut free and change the subject. 'Do you enjoy advertising?' I asked.

'Sometimes, yes,' he replied equally glad to be off the hook. 'But it can be very stressful. It has given me an ulcer.'

'Really? How long have you been working in the business?'

'About six months.'

Sleep was waiting for me in my hotel room which even my cough could not disturb, but I was disturbed by the account director. He called me at what felt like two in the morning.

'Please, Kneeel, have you done advertisement for television?' he asked.

'No.'

'Oh.' There was a pause. 'So what will you present tomorrow?'

I felt like saying 'my backside'. Instead I reassured him: 'Don't worry. I'll do some work first thing.'

'Excellent. Thank you. But please do me a favour.'

'What?'

'Don't make the idea too expensive.'

Traffic Diversions

'India is the world's largest potential market. A middle class of over two hundred million starved of choice. Virgin territory. The *Big One!*' the multinational bosses yell from behind their stretched desks in Tokyo, Frankfurt, London and New York. Mind you, should any of these bosses ever visit The *Big One* they will invariably limit their stay to a couple of days during the temperate winter, take in the Taj Mahal in an air-conditioned limousine, be entertained with a lavish dinner and leave with a couple of Kashmiri silk carpets as souvenirs and virtually no idea about how business is conducted, or electrocuted, in the Indian subcontinent.

In some respects these distant potentates are right, however. India is slowly, even reluctantly a few might argue, becoming The *Big One*. Currently, it is the world's fifth largest economy but it has far more potential for growth than the five above it—China, perhaps, excluded. There is a vast middle class with an increasingly disposable income and a craving for Westernized brands rather than anonymous commodities. Labour is cheap and plentiful in almost every part of the country and thanks to Nehru's policies there is a large pool of technological and scientific expertise as well as a stable industrial base. But most important of all, since 1992, the government has demonstrated its commitment to liberalizing the economy by removing many of the Draconian tariffs and restrictions, and making the rupee convertible for trade purposes.

That's the good news.

The bad news was that all this good news had yet to reach my clients. They still behaved like myopic moghuls; relying on a hunch rather than research or outside advice, switching products in midstream, disappearing 'out of station' for weeks on end, ignoring invoices and generally treating their agency like a sandwich-board man.

It was after presenting to one of our most eccentric clients that I realized I might be in the right universe but I was definitely on the wrong planet. This client produced coir mattresses as thin as an After Eight Mint and about as comfortable to sleep on. I had written the line FOR THE REST OF YOUR LIFE and underlined REST to get the pun across. Because the agency lacked a photocopier—leasing one was a decision my Indian partner spent six months wrestling over—Vikki had used a copy shop nearby and inadvertently left a sample behind. Somehow this lost copy had fallen into the wrong hands. When I started to present I was informed by the client that the line had recently been used by a rival.

'It was our idea first,' I protested. 'We'll sue them.'

Everyone laughed. In India, unless you're Rip Van Winkle, you don't sue anybody. So clogged up are the courts it can take years, sometimes as many as fifty, to reach a verdict.

We were in the client's house in Vasant Vihar, one of Delhi's more exclusive, southern suburbs. The drawing room where we were presenting looked like the departure lounge to heaven. Gold wardrobes lined two of the walls, a vast crystal chandelier contained enough bulbs to illuminate a stadium and a huge, badly carved statue of Eros offered guests a final cigarette from a box stuck on the end of the arrow. On second thoughts, maybe it was the departure lounge to hell, because while I was trying to present the client's grandson ran round the room screaming at the top of his voice.

They were a husband and wife team, both in their seventies. He wore a uniform but she clearly wore the belt. Her English was better than his but she still gave the impression that she was taking it for a test drive. Oddly, whenever he addressed me he called me 'Doctor'.

I had presented two advertisements. Neither of them liked either. After a lengthy discussion, mainly in Hindi, I was informed the work was too Western.

'Try again, doctor,' I was told. And then I was given a cup of something hot and sweet, perhaps in order to Indianize my creativity.

'Well, where do we go from here?' one of my colleagues anxiously asked as we climbed into his car. I knew where I was going: back to bed.

I've had some of my best ideas while in bed. Awake, that is. Not asleep. I'm of the opinion that being horizontal allows the creative juices to flow more liberally. Some of the ancient Greeks believed that ideas were fermented in the testicles and then transferred to the brain. By lying down I had less gravity to fight. But not all my employers have shared this enthusiasm. At one London agency I dispensed with my desk, filing cabinet and chairs and installed a red, antique dentist's chair. When fully reclined I was almost horizontal. Unfortunately, such was the uncontrollable heat in my office, plus the convenience of a pub next door where anything less than a four pint lunch was considered unreasonable, that come the afternoon I often dozed off—leaving my mouth wide open and unwittingly inviting a full dental inspection from my excitable superior.

In Delhi no one seemed to care where my ideas came from or even if they were my ideas. Had I been less conscientious I could have survived for months recycling advertisements from Peruvian or Russian award annuals; assuming, that is, I could understand them in the first place. But I wanted to be original. Well, using one of my old ideas that had never seen the light of day would be acceptable. Lying in bed, exhausted by the heat and my still alien environment, I ransacked my memory to see if I could find a suitable leftover for the coir mattress company. Within minutes I had fallen asleep.

I was woken by the phone ringing.

'Hello?' I answered.

'Mr Ketty?' enquired a distant voice wrapped in static.

'Kelly. Yes?'

The caller explained that he was calling from our Bombay office, that he was the general manager there and needed my creative help urgently.

'I'm kind of busy at the moment,' I explained. And tired. 'I have to finish some ads for a mattress client.'

'We have such a client?'He sounded surprised.

'If we don't I'm starting to hallucinate.'

'But this is very important project otherwise I would not be bothering you,' he insisted. 'It's for—'

He was interrupted by the hotel's switchboard.

'Excuse me sir,' said the operator. 'I have a call for you from Bombay.'

'What? I am . . . I was already talking to Bombay.' I pointed out. There was a pause then my original caller returned.

'What happened there?' he asked.

'No idea.'

'Anyway,' he resumed. 'This project is for one of our top clients, an insurance company.'

Insurance companies—along with banks, investment institutions and hotels—invariably ended up being a creative man's nadir. They always wanted advertisements that made their chairmen feel good rather than the consumers. 'Warm Bath' advertising. Comforting but soggy. I groaned.

'Are you okay?'

'Just my career rubbing against the bottom,' I joked. 'So what kind of campaign do they want?'

'They want a road safety campaign.'

My groan became a laugh. Road safety? In India? From the short time I had been in the country that had to be one of the world's great oxymorons. This was a land where basic traffic rules were seemingly ignored, wildly experimented with or never understood in the first place. A red traffic light could mean stop or charge. Come darkness and many drivers launched a surprise attack by driving around without any lights. Others made a deliberate point of driving on the wrong side of the road. Perhaps they were aware of a secret master plan to remove another vestige of the country's colonial past and switch to driving on the right hand side of the road.

The only rule apparently followed by one and all in this, The First Great Traffic War, was that small vehicles should give way to larger vehicles unless they wanted to become even smaller. When those of a similar size did combat it all came down to whose nerve went first and who could hoot the longest and loudest. For the horn was patently a driver's most powerful ammunition and the art of staying alive on India's roads was to forget there was anything behind and honk everything in front. After all, the rear view mirror was only installed as a hook for some fluffy ornament or to check that the driver's hair, make-up or even head was still in place. There was something sublimely existential about this philosophy: I hoot therefore I am. And the bigger the vehicle the bigger the hoot and the claim to exist. Trucks and buses sounded like crazed elephants while at the other end of the fuel chain auto-rickshaws and scooters squeaked like terrified mice. Unlike the West—hoot someone in the States and they might blow you away—no one seemed to take offence if you honked them. Everyone was trying to prove they existed. Trucks even begged for it by having HORN PLEASE emblazoned across their backs.

So, after a few weeks in India, this much I knew: no one was safe on the roads and any sensible driver would buy a horn with a car rather than the other way round.

'A road safety campaign?' I repeated to the general manager in Bombay. 'That's a superhuman task. Currently, I feel half human.'

'I understand,' he replied. 'It's the heat, I'm sure. Relax and I'll fax the brief to your office.'

I was getting unwillingly roped in. Then I remembered. My office fax was out of order.

*

The traffic in Cairo was at times worse than Delhi's although perhaps a shade safer. It is the only city I've visited where I was involved in a traffic jam at three in the morning. One evening the agency boss invited me round for dinner. He lived in the penthouse of an otherwise empty apartment block with his Californian wife and an English butler. There were two other guests present: a senior army officer and a Yorkshireman who had been banished to Cairo, or so he maintained, because he couldn't pronounce the name of the company he worked for, Schweppes. He made is lispishly sound like Sweps. The army officer was in charge of the Board of Censors before which every commercial had to be aired. As we sipped our cocktails he asked me whether I had noticed how bad the traffic was in the city. I said I had. He then asked if I would produce, as 'a present', a campaign to stop people using their vehicles unless absolutely necessary.

'If we do this for him,' my host later explained, 'he will approve all our commercials. But since we'll have to pay for the cost of production try to keep the concept simple.'

In other words, don't make the idea too expensive.

I tried to protest that I had come to Cairo to work on a number of specific projects and that ridding the roads of traffic was not one of them.

'Do it for me,' his six foot Barbie doll of a wife cooed.

For her, especially after two bottles of exceptionally fine wine, I would have hammered a six inch nail into my head; a task which, on reflection, would have been marginally more enjoyable than the one she persuaded me to embark upon.

After several days of concentration, more on her than the traffic, I came up with a three A's campaign. Alert, Alarm and Advise. Such natty thinking is usually the last resort of a desperate adman and I was no exception. Through a series of cheap commercials I intended to alert the population about how the traffic was polluting their ancient city, alarm them with statistics—which since I couldn't find any I made up—and finally advise them to use public transport.

'No! No! No!' the army officer unhappily responded after I had shown him the work. 'You have not solved the problem.'

I was leaving the following day so what did I care? But I pointed out to him that three specialist teams from Los Angeles, Bangkok and Tokyo had spent months and millions trying to solve the problem and become as snarled up as the traffic.

'You could always double the price of petrol,' I finally suggested.

'What? And start a riot!'

If anyone out there wants a campaign to promote civil unrest, I'm the man.

*

Despite my office fax being out of order the brief for the road safety campaign mysteriously appeared on my desk. It was a brief for an almighty challenge although longer than 'Please produce advertisement to sell television.' I decided my Alert, Alarm and Advise approach could be fashioned to fit. This time, however, I intended to use real statistics instead of imaginary ones. But statistics, reliable ones, proved hard to come by and no two sources seemed able to agree. Even the country's population total was open to debate. Eventually, I discovered around 59,000 were killed on the roads the previous year, including 3,000 in Delhi where a

further 10,000 had been seriously injured. This made the capital not only the hottest place on earth but also the most dangerous.

In the name of research I decided to experience the dangers of the road first hand. Those I talked to suggested the road to Agra. My own worldwide chairman had been on that road a year before along with his wife. After a hair-raising trip she had wound the window down as they waited at a level crossing for a train to pass. Suddenly a basket had appeared. The lid was thrown back and a cobra rose inches from her face. Traumatized, she was shipped back to the States.

Um and his car had been requisitioned so I hired a similar chicken soup Ambassador from the hotel. It came with a smartly uniformed Sikh driver who said his name was Harrikat. At last, a name I could pronounce. As we set off, horn blasting at anything that moved, he announced that to survive on the roads of India 'you need good brakes, good horn and good luck.' About an hour later he stopped, opened the bonnet and told me that we were out of brake fluid. Thankfully, we were not out of luck or without a horn.

By leaving at dawn it was alarming to see how many things had gone bump in the night and the worst casualties—apparently offenders, too—were the top-heavy trucks which lay smashed as if thrown down by a petulant giant.

'See, truck drivers drink plenty at night,' was Harrikat's explanation for the carnage.

It was a disturbing notion. 'What do they drink?' I asked. With yet another truck homing in on us, headlights flashing, horn blowing, I wasn't sure I wanted to know the answer.

'Thunderbolt, mainly. Super strong beer.'

A sort of alcoholic diesel which does to the human mind what dynamite does to a building.

'Don't they fall asleep at the wheel? Drink makes you sleepy. It's a depressant,' I said.

'They take pills, also. Lots of pills. Amphetamines.'

Speed! God knows what kind of weirdness they were seeing through their bug-coated windscreens.

Squashed cars and overturned trucks marked our journey like milestones that morning. There was never any evidence of drivers or passengers. Just a circle of stones placed around each abandoned wreck like a grave. At one point we passed a dead cow lying on its side, also ringed with stones.

Harrikat shook his head at the sight. 'If you kill an animal in this country it can cost you many rupees,' he said.

'You mean you're fined?'

'No, the villagers will get very angry and demand compensation.'

Kill one of their children and it can prove considerably more expensive. A European businessman staying at the hotel told me how his car had once accidently and tragically hit a child running across the highway late at night. In compensation his company had to build the village a new school. Life may be cheap in India but death can be expensive.

*

I justified my death-defying trip to Agra by taking in the Taj Mahal, the jewel and marble masterpiece designed by Shah Jahan in memory of his wife who had died giving birth to his fourteenth child. A tomb for a womb. It took a work force of 20,000 over twenty years to build but by the time I came to visit, almost four centuries later, the acidic effects of pollution were starting to unbuild it. Also it was smaller than I had imagined, though Harrikat, who had switched from driver to guide, pointed out that it had probably looked bigger when it was built.

'I don't follow,' I said.

'People were shorter then,' he reasoned.

I had reserved a room at the Taj View Hotel but either the hotel or the view had moved. Instead of a moonlit, marble mausoleum I was rewarded with the sight of a primeval pond which had once been a swimming pool.

'Where's my view?' I rang and asked, I assumed, a man at the front desk.

There was a pause. 'I am not knowing the question, sir.'

'When I made my reservation in Delhi I specifically asked for a room with a view of the Taj Mahal,' I slowly explained turning each word into a mantra.

'Sir, I'm thinking you dialled wrong number. This room service.'

A few minutes later I dialled him again. This time deliberately. I was hungry. 'Forget the view,' I told the same voice. 'Can I please order a club sandwich?'

I had left one hotel room for another and in hotel rooms there's not much else to do than to bond with the bed. Since it was a fond hobby of mine I willingly stretched out and reviewed my life in India so far. Besides being barbecued by the heat and discovering the innumerous permutations of a gin and tonic I hadn't achieved too much. My ideas for the television company in Old Delhi had proved too expensive and unless I cracked the coir mattress campaign I suspected the client would go in search of another 'doctor'. Now I had the meaning of life to wrestle with: Road Safety in India. It was a task as daunting as the electrification of the Soviet Union. I closed my eyes and hoped it would go away.

There was an indecent irony at play. Here I was trying to sell a mattress and bring safety to the roads of India but I couldn't nod off because of the traffic noise outside. To complete the irony I turned on the television. It wasn't showing better programmes. On one station prime minister Rao was attending some kind of function. He had his eyes closed. Perhaps he hoped all his problems would go away, too.

*

If the drive to Agra had been hair-raising the even longer trip back home was cardiac-arresting. It was as if the outgoing journey had been a dress rehearsal and to make matters worse it started raining.

'Put your wipers on,' I told Harrikat as his windscreen became opaque from the torrential downpour.

'Wiper doesn't work,' he replied. The Grim Reaper now had all the trump cards. But Harrikat was a resourceful man. To compensate for the lack of wipers he drove with his head stuck out of the window as suicidal trucks and buses thundered past. I arrived at my hotel a mental wreck determined never to drive or be driven out of the city again.

That evening while calming my nerves with several large gin and tonics in the hotel bar—domestic doubles with lemon—I fell into conversation with an American software salesman from Houston, Texas. He asked me what I was doing in India and I told him I was working for an ad agency. I also told him I was trying to come up with a campaign to promote road safety.

'That's funny,' he said the way Americans do, even if you've just revealed that your wife had run off with a neighbour and your only child had been kidnapped by Afghan rebels. 'You've sure got a difficult job. But at least you're British.'

'What's that got to do with it?'

'I remember the first time I came here—six, seven years ago. Middle of the night. Hot as Hell!' he replied. 'I got a cab from the airport to this hotel. Journey took about half an hour. Absolute nightmare! Guy went through every red light, almost hit a cow in the fast lane and then began weaving across the road. I thought he'd fallen asleep so I tapped him on the shoulder. "Hey, fella," I said. "Why d'ya think they put them white lines on the road?" The driver shrugged. "Don't know, sir," he said. "They were left behind by the British."'

The Single Cell Cafe

My contract, negotiated during my brief February visit and finally sealed back in the States through a series of fragmented faxes, stipulated a company car and driver. However, my vision of dashing through downtown Delhi in a chauffeur driven Mercedes melted once I arrived, like everything else in the summer heat. For a start Delhi doesn't have a downtown. It's all over the place. Also, the car which eventually appeared about a week after my trip to Agra was a four-year-old, chicken soup Premier driven up from our sister agency in Bombay.

I can only assume the car was given its primigenial name because it must be the first to be conceived by an Italian, designed by a Russian, engineered by a Japanese and assembled by an Indian. It would not, had I been given a selection to pick from, have been my first choice.

The Premier is a small car so it made sense that the driver hired to drive it should be one of the largest men in India. Previously he had been a professional boxer, a soldier fighting in Kashmir, a foreman in Iraq and a bus driver in Delhi. He spoke English fluently, although his name sounded Portuguese: George D'Souza. Once he squeezed himself into the driver's seat the Premier leaned dangerously over and we travelled around like a small yacht tacking against a gale force wind.

On the first day of his employment he appeared with long sideburns and a thick crop of jet black hair which he openly admitted to dyeing. Come the second day he appeared looking like a marine.

'You've had a haircut, George,' I remarked stating the obvious.

'Yes, sir,' he replied, obviously not at all happy with the result. 'Barber says my hair is angry with me. So he cut most of it off. Now there is less hair to be angry.'

Besides having angry hair George had a voracious appetite and a chronic case of hypochondria. He was always hungry and always sick. Whenever there was a pause in our schedule I could see him battling with the dilemma of which to visit first: a food stall or the chemists.

'I am a very big man,' he never tired of telling me. 'I must eat or my muscles will turn into flab.' Eating was his idea of doing exercise. Eating and talking. As we drove, tilted around Delhi, he talked endlessly about his past, his family, India, money (his eternal lack of it) and his ill health. He also wasted many words telling me how I deserved a better car than the Premier; more to the point, I suspect, how he deserved to drive a better car than the Premier.

'Listen George,' I cautioned, 'be grateful for small mercies. They could have given me a Maruti.'

When Maruti Udyog and the Japanese company, Suzuki, joined together to produce an 800cc tin box, it became an overnight success. Umpteen thousands now buzz along India's roads like tormented mosquitoes and many end up being swatted or squashed by a larger adversary. Given the lack of protection Marutis offer and the wild and crazy way in which they're driven—these were the first ever domestically produced cars to provide the thrill of acceleration—it is reasonable to suppose their owners entered into some kind of Faustian deal whereby they exchanged their brains in order to obtain one. And as if to prove they no longer possess their minds they place inane stickers on their car's backsides. KAR FOLKS. MUSIC CAR. KAR COOL. CAR SHOPPE. KIT CAR. KAR-O-BAR. CAR-N-STYLE. HELLO CAR. CAR TODAY. CAR AGE. The last two are the most meaningful even if incomplete. Should be CAR TODAY, WRECK TOMORROW. And add an N to the middle of CAR AGE; for that is what they cause and become as they weave, race and swerve.

In short, Marutis are driven by Marunatics.

Or as George put it with great disdain: 'They're driven by puppies.'

'Puppies?'

'Punjabi yuppies,' he elaborated.

I should explain that George was not well disposed towards his fellow countrymen, especially if they were successful. His father, an Anglo-Indian, had been a prominent lawyer but died when his son was young and his wealth had passed to the sister in Calcutta for reasons George never conveyed. When not hungry, sick or talking George would write begging letters to his aunt asking for funds for his own family of six.

'I know she never gets the letters and I can't afford to visit her.'

'Why wouldn't she get the letters?' I asked ignoring his less than subtle plea for a free air ticket to Calcutta.

'The government opens them. Here they open all letters.'

I subsequently found out he was partly right. Some letters do get opened, particularly if it is obvious that they contain something inside besides paper. It is considered the postman's perk. But why anyone would open and steal a begging letter, in George's case probably hundreds of begging letters, was hard to imagine.

Certainly, the thick manila envelopes that started landing on my office desk had not been opened. They contained glossy brochures for expensive foreign cars which I eventually found out George had instructed dealers to send me.

'You're going to have to learn to love the Premier,' I told him. 'The agency can't afford a foreign car. Nor can I.'

'But it is bad for your image, sir,' he persisted.

If I had an image in India it was fuzzy and underexposed. Nor had it been helped by a journalist printing an off the record quote—supposed to be a humorous quip—that I had left the States to come to India because 'I was living my career in reverse.'

George played his trump card. 'Also, sir, this car is not safe.'

'Not safe in what way?'

'Parts keep falling off.'

'What parts?'

'Important parts.'

I'd had enough of what I suspected was yet another ruse to get me to change my car. 'In that case it's your job to put them back on, or stop them falling off in the first place.'

'Yes, sir,' he accepted with a forlorn look.

Though George did not care for the Premier he normally drove with care; his avoirdupois prevented us from going too fast, anyway. But driving to work one morning he suddenly swerved violently and , from where I was sitting, for no apparent reason.

'What happened?' I asked.

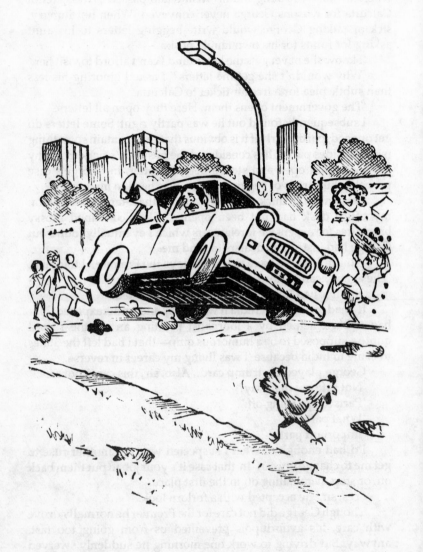

'Sir, there was a rag on the road.'

'A rag?' I looked out of the rear window expecting to see a rag the size of a rolled-up carpet. Instead, all I could see was a piece of blue cloth the size of a handkerchief flapping around in our wake. 'I hardly think that would have damaged the car,' I said sarcastically.

'No, sir. But it could have killed us.'

He went on to explain how it was an old superstition—and George, naturally, believed in old superstitions. If someone in a family was dying from a disease they wiped a rag over that family member and placed it on the road. Whoever drove over it picked up the disease and left the other person cured.

'Sounds like a load of old codswallop to me,' I said sceptically.

The following day I fell ill.

*

The hotel's doctor who came to visit me resembled an Indian version of Ralph Lauren and, as if to confirm the likeness, was dressed from head to toe in heavily branded fake Polo garments. Walking past the wall mirror he paused, checked his appearance, patted his oiled hair and smiled at the result. The dapper doc.

'So, what's wrong with you?' he asked moving a chair to my bedside.

'I don't know,' I answered. 'That's why I called you.'

'Excellent decision,' he agreed. His eyes wandered across the room and finally rested on my electronic typewriter. 'Let's begin by taking your temperature,' he suggested. In my semi-delirium I thought for a moment he had said 'typewriter' instead of 'temperature'.

Zipping open his leather handbag he pulled out a thermometer and a couple of minutes later informed me I was running a very high temperature; that my hair was plastered down with sweat and my skin was hotter than a Delhi road only confirmed his diagnosis.

'Are your bowel movements regular?' he went on to enquire.

'I think I've counted every tile in the bathroom a zillion times.'

He let out a short, designed laugh which he completed with a neat cough. 'How long have you been in India?'

I tried to remember, but time had taken another handful of valium. 'About two months,' I guessed.

'You arrived at the wrong time of the year. Far too hot. Your system is finding it hard to acclimatize.'

'If my system includes my brain you're dead right.'

He smiled. 'We'll start at the bottom and work up. I need a stool sample.' He pulled a small, plastic container out of his handbag. 'I'll have someone come over later and pick it up.' This conjured up a curious image of some anonymous peon riding through the night in a ramshackle auto-rickshaw clutching a sick foreigner's scatological souvenir.

Before leaving the doctor walked over and took a closer look at my typewriter. 'Did you buy this in India?'

'No. Hong Kong.'

'Very compact,' he said picking it up. 'Very light.' He held it in mid-air as if expecting me to say: 'Oh, go on, take it.'

He returned the following evening dressed to heal in another mock Polo combination and, as before, perused his reflection in the wall mirror before taking a seat. 'It is as I expected,' he said. 'You're suffering from amoebic dysentery.'

'Amoebic dysentery?'

'It's very common this time of the year. The heat and lack of hygiene. Just drink lots of water to avoid dehydration and take these medicines.' He took three packets out of his handbag. 'Anyway, you're looking better,' he lied.

'I feel worse. Much worse.'

'It really is only a severe case of food poisoning. You'll be fine in a couple of days,' he tried to reassure me while giving the typewriter another longing glance. Maybe he hoped I would leave it to him in my will.

Food poisoning, or Delhi Belly, or Revenge for the Raj seems to be India's way of saying 'HI' to newcomers. As I lay in bed becoming half the man I used to be I thought back to my most recent meals trying to decide which one had been responsible. The sweet and sour pork in a Chinese restaurant seemed the most likely candidate. To speed my convalescence I started dreaming up unbearably painful tortures to inflict on the management by way of revenge.

Living in the world's largest Indian restaurant can be a mixed blessing and after so many biryanis and tandooris I began craving for another country's cuisine. Because there are very few foreign restaurants in Delhi I ended up eating Chinese more by default than desire. I had originally ordered fish. There were a variety of fish dishes on the menu, all labelled specials of the house, but every one I requested was off, according to the waiter who was about as Chinese as a cheeseburger. 'Off' didn't necessarily mean unavailable, however. When I pressed the waiter for an explanation why there were no special fish dishes he proudly announced: 'In India, sir, all fish is polluted.' So I ordered pork and proved pigs can fly—right through me.

*

My first visitor from the outside world was a bald and bearded Bengali art director from the office. Gosh, I had nicknamed him, because I never ceased to be amazed over how fast he could speak—hundreds of words a minute. If challenged I was sure he could recite the entire Ramayana in under an hour. Given the speed at which he spoke most of what he said was incomprehensible. I would grab the odd recognizable word and attempt to construct a new sentence.

'Amoebic . . . father . . . forever . . .'

'So your father could never get rid of his amoeba?' I tried to summarize.

'Liver . . . brain . . . no cure . . .'

I gave up, I preferred to suffer in ignorance. 'How's work?' I eventually asked hoping a change of subject might produce a more cogent response. Not so. If anything he began to speak even faster.

'Crazy . . . problems . . . emergency . . . resigned . . . .' I let him rattle on towards Armageddon, closed my eyes and dreamed up further reprisals to inflict upon the chef at the Chinese restaurant.

George also came to visit me. He was wearing an extremely tight, dark suit and off-white training shoes. As a further gesture to the formality of the occasion he had attempted to tame his angry hair with a generous dab of Brylcreem—a product which sells extremely well in Indonesia, I was once told, where it is used as a sandwich spread. Whether as a gift or an omen he placed a prayer book on the bedside table. 'Me and the family are all praying for you, sir.'

'I appreciate that but I think I'm going to live. I've only got amoebic dysentery.'

He shook his head in concern. 'I've had that, sir. In the army. You get this amoeboid inside you and it grows and grows and grows.' He stretched his arms out until I was carrying an amoeba the size of a labrador.

'Is that right?'

'Yes, sir. It's horrible. You need to drink lassi. Lots of it.'

'I don't like lassi.'

'I'll get the wife to make some tonight. Bring it in tomorrow.' He fell silent for awhile. 'Frankly, sir, I haven't been too well myself.'

'I'm sorry to hear that.'

'I keep thinking perhaps I didn't miss that rag on the road. It happened to a cousin of the wife's. He turned yellow and couldn't stop shaking. He never completely recovered.'

'You'll be fine.' The last thing I needed were two patients in the same room.

'Of course, sir, I could be suffering from the thunder disease,' he went on, determined to be afflicted with some kind of ailment.

'The thunder disease? I've never heard of it.'

'That driver you call Um, he told me about it. It's a sort of infectious depression. He says you catch it from miserable people.'

'I think he's winding you up,' I said manufacturing a yawn. 'Anyway, thanks for coming to see me, George. You've really cheered me up.'

'It's been a pleasure, sir,' he said missing the irony. 'I'll be back tomorrow with the lassi.'

I did eventually recover and without having to drink lassi. I looked different, though. Less hair and face. Thinner all over. Not only was my career slowly disappearing, so was I.

India's Not Broken, It's Under Repair

My hotel bill was rapidly becoming the agency's largest account. I had to find a home of my own. While Delhi's rents and property prices are not quite so high as in Bombay—now the world's most expensive, even more so than Tokyo or New York—they still hover around the astronomic. Furthermore, most deals are complicated and illicit involving vast sums of a hard currency being exchanged under the table for a roof over the head. And, in the case of renting, the landlord invariably demands up to two year's rent in advance.

The excessive demand, and demands, for accommodation has created a shadowy world of unscrupulous fixers, touts and brokers. I have been told there are more brokers in Delhi, over six hundred in the southern suburbs alone, than anywhere else on the planet. Another doubtful first for the capital.

Mr J.P.Singh, the broker I had been recommended by the office, told me he had 'a BA in Real Estate from Florida University'. In contrast to Gosh he spoke very, very slowly and very precisely, as if under the assumption that English was not my first language.

'So, which part of town do you desire to reside in, Mr Kay Lee?'

I had been living in Delhi long enough by then to appreciate that being well-addressed was of critical importance. The cachet of the right address could turn a business card into a credit card; even, I hoped, my business card. Such were the attacks on our cash flow and the lack of new business opportunities that I was looking for a neighbour who could end up being a client, or at least put me in touch with potential clients. 'Call it a shrewd business move,' I said to my Indian partner. He stared blankly back at me. But then he had started staring at me a lot recently.

There were four possible areas where I initially felt I might be able to achieve my objective. The first was Puppieland. Most of the Puppies had gravitated to the newer enclaves and colonies like

Greater Kailash, Panchsheel Park and Defence Colony where they sipped smuggled French wine, raced their Maruti mosquitoes and consumed hours of satellite television. But Puppies were more my market than my mentors. They were The *Big One's* emerging middle class. To succeed I had to be more upwardly mobile.

Dipland was the second possibility. Dipland was where the diplomats lived: in Vasant Vihar, West End, Shanti Niketan or, if they could afford it, Lodi Estate, Jor Bagh and Golf Links. However, after considering this option it did not appear viable. Diplomats—even though some were little more than civil servants with passports—tended to keep to themselves in a perpetual state of alcoholic immunity, and while a few expatriate businessmen had infiltrated their ranks my chances of moving next door to one were slim.

Then there was Garboland, 'I want to be alone' land. Here antisocialites had moved out beyond the city limits and bought or rented designer boxes in the scrub, on the desert's edge, which they euphemistically called farms. But the only animals they kept were guard dogs and the only crop a well pampered lawn. It was all too remote to become intimate unless I wanted a Howard Hughes for a client.

The city's and country's elite—senior politicians and civil servants, generals of soldiers and captains of industry, successful speculators and property tycoons plus a sprinkling of ambassadors (people not cars) and occasionally resident NRIs (non-resident Indians)—lived in Powerland, the exclusive area around Akbar Road and the very heart of the capital. These were the people who were too powerful to suffer power cuts and who mixed Johnny Walker Black Label with favours and intrigues. Although already well enough protected by their social and political positions these superlative citizens insisted on protecting themselves still further with close circuit television cameras, dogs the size of donkeys, floodlights, barbed wire and round the clock armed chowkidars keeping guard. By hook or by being a crook many of them had risen to the top of one of the world's toughest societies and no one was going to take it away from them or them away from it.

This was obviously the area of town I should be living in.

*

The White House was a new block of apartments already turning grey on the perimeter of Powerland. As we drove in through the gates J.P.Singh told me it was a unique block.

'Blocks of flats are extremely rare in Delhi,' he explained. 'And this is a luxury block. It offers its residents a swimming pool, health club, cable television hook-up, twenty-four hour security and even has its own power supply.' He paused to let all these amenities sink in, then added with a sagacious nod of his head: 'Several film stars are living here.'

This sounded encouraging. I knew that in India film stars were close to deity, the ultimate name drop. With these kind of neighbours I would have clients begging to be serviced by our agency. Though, to be honest, when I looked up at the stained block every floor appeared empty.

'It looks empty,' I said.

'Looks can be deceptive,' J.P. Singh enigmatically replied. 'Come, let us look at your new home.'

What was really unique about the White House, I discovered once I had moved in, was that it was still being built while simultaneously falling apart. Additionally, while planning permission had been granted for an eight storey block in their excitement the builders had added four extra floors, creating a deluge of writs, injunctions and the imminent possibility of the entire building being demolished. Of course, none of this was disclosed as J.P. Singh enthusiastically showed me round a flat on the first floor. Undecorated, naked, anonymous it could have been in Hong Kong or Cairo. The only fixture was an ornate and vulgar crystal chandelier hanging from the centre of the living room. Thankfully, it was not as large as the one which had been hanging in the coir mattress man's celestial departure lounge.

'The landlord told me he will be leaving this here,' J.P. Singh said of the chandelier.

'Wise man,' I replied.

Missing or ignoring my sarcasm he wrenched open the french windows to the balcony. One of them detached itself from the runners and, despite the subsequent efforts of a score of workmen, would never properly close again.

'Pleasant view,' he suggested. For several, silent moments we both stood staring at a few dying trees and the obvious embryonic makings of a large and permanent slum. 'Don't worry about the jhuggi,' he for once quickly added. 'The workers who built the building live there. Now the building is finished, they'll go.' But it wasn't and they didn't.

Observing poverty so close to home, literally hanging over it, left me with a hollow feeling. I was reminded of something Mark Tully had written in an introduction to one of his books. When asked by a visitor how he coped with the poverty he replied: 'I don't have to. The poor do.'

'Aren't there any flats on a higher floor ?' I asked. 'If I'm going to live in a tower block I'd prefer to have a more panoramic view.'

'I'm afraid not. This is a very prestigious address.' Then he added in a typical salesman's style and ever so ever so slowly, 'This is the last flat available. You must decide now or it will be snapped up by someone else.'

'Let me see the pool,' I said.

'Of course.'

We returned to the lobby which looked more like a building site and crossed over to the swimming pool. Half full, its surface was covered with a veneer of dead insects. A muscular young man in shorts wandered over to greet us. 'Hello, I'm lifeguard,' he proudly announced.

'Good. So if I start drowning you can save me,' I joked.

He looked perplexed and exchanged a glance with J.P. Singh. 'Not so, sir. I cannot swim.'

Another contradiction. Another indication that I should have looked elsewhere for my dream home.

'Come and see the health club,' the broker urged. 'It has all the latest equipment imported from the States.'

The sign on the door said HEALTH CLUB but that was the only clue. For the room we stepped into, windowless and hot, was conspicuously empty. 'There's nothing here,' I said.

J.P. Singh looked around, then walked around. He tapped one of the walls as if hoping to find a secret door behind which all the equipment had gone into hiding. 'Most odd,' he said more to himself. He turned to the lifeguard and, I guess, demanded an explanation in Hindi. The lifeguard talked for five or so minutes. 'There's been some delay, apparently because of the paperwork. However, he assures me it will be fully operational by the time you move in,' J.P. Singh eventually translated.

I had foolishly assumed I could move into my power pad within a few days. Instead, it took over two months. The primary cause of the delay was the malfunctioning air-conditioning. These were new split units and, to be fair, they were installed a couple of days after signing the lease. They may even have initially worked, but a cleaner pulled one of them away from the wall so he could clean the floor underneath and most of the coolant shot out over the entire apartment and the fuse box burst into flames. The only positive side of the resulting electrical fire was that the donated chandelier melted. It had been made of plastic not crystal.

If the cleaner couldn't clean I was about to be visited by an electrician who had most of his wires crossed. In any society there are cowboys who ride carelessly from one job to the next. In India, I suspect, they sometimes ride out of one kind of vocation into another, completely unrelated one. A man wakes up, sits bolt upright in bed and declares with the conviction of a visionary: 'Today, I'm going to be an electrician!' Yesterday he was possibly a plumber and the day before that a car mechanic or even an advertising executive. This occupational dexterity, besides adding to the daily anarchy, can give rise to what I call the game of Indian Roulette.

Allow many months to play Indian Roulette. I only allowed two. Besides time the game requires at least six other players and a faulty appliance; for example, an air-conditioner, or several. It is extremely unlikely that the other six players will arrive to play the game at the same time. That is not how it works. In my case the first player to appear was the born-again electrician who spent an age replacing the burnt out wiring and repairing the fuse box. When he had finished the power came in surges and produced that awful, pervasive smell of electric fish. This, he concluded, was the fault of the junction box which couldn't handle the power load.

To check out the junction box involved the landlord. Since he was away in Europe, wisely avoiding the Delhi heat while spending my substantial deposit, the game was suspended until his son was eventually contacted. When he arrived he vehemently maintained the junction box was brand new, state of the art, and the real cause of my problems was that insufficient power was coming into the apartment block.

At this point the game became swamped. The manager of the building, a colossal Bihari, appeared with a host of faces from DESU—the Delhi power company. They hotly debated the issue at length but not in English. At which point Krishnan, the office manager, arrived. Acting as translator he told me there was nothing apparently wrong with the power supply—except that it kept failing—and the fault lay with the units.

The next player, the retailer from whom the units had been purchased, declined to play until a few legal threats were thrown into the game. On arriving he inspected his units by gently stroking them like a pet while murmuring what sounded like some kind of mantra. He completed his strange ritual but refused to accept responsibility and instead blamed the installer. I think it was about this point in the game that I accepted I would probably be living in a hotel throughout my stay in India. If nothing else it had air-conditioning.

A posse of installers duly arrived and allowed more coolant to ejaculate over the newly repainted walls. They were keen to apportion the blame to everyone and anyone. When pressed to be more precise they said the wrong kind of power points had been fitted. Back came another born-again electrician who jabbed a borrowed screwdriver into one of the power points and fused not only my flat but the entire building. 'There!' he exclaimed triumphantly. 'Building has been badly designed.'

So, I had been given six shots at the truth. All I had to do was hold the barrel to my temple, spin the chamber and squeeze the trigger. I could have been dead right with the outcome, or dead wrong.

'In India everyone experiments with the truth,' Krishnan, the office manager, told me. Indeed, Mahatma Gandhi gave his autobiography the title: THE STORY OF MY EXPERIMENTS WITH TRUTH, though nowhere does he mention air-conditioning. J.P. Singh had certainly carried out a nuclear experiment with the truth. Not only were there no film stars living in the White House there were only two other tenants, and one was caretaking for an absent doctor. The other, an elderly woman, ran for cover whenever she saw me. With my 'shrewd business move' it seemed I had successfully checkmated myself.

One morning Krishnan informed me that my chilling machines were finally working.

'No longer broken? That's excellent news,' I told him.

'They weren't broken, just under repair,' he corrected me. At least his was a more optimistic interpretation of the truth.

It Won't Work Here

While waiting for my apartment to become habitable I had spent the weekends attempting to dress its hot nakedness. My forays into consumerism made the term 'Shopping Expedition' seem particularly appropriate, for in Delhi the concept of a shopping mall is still a wink in the retailer's eye. Instead, those born to shop have a limited choice of several markets, the majority of which look identical—a three-sided square with a patch of scorched earth in the middle—and all offer a very similar selection of shops and products: hardware, mainly. Occasionally I would stumble across a department store but invariably it only had one department . . . selling hardware.

At Khan Market, the Eldorado of Delhi's markets, George and I found a television, one of the eight million colour sets in India. To keep it company I also bought a stereo system. The stereo was called: THE POWERHOUSE 320 DBB.

'What does DBB stand for?' I asked the shop assistant.

'Dynamic Bass Boost,' he answered. 'Makes music very thumpy.'

'Thumpy?'

'Yes, sir.'

But when I bought a few cassettes to play on the POWERHOUSE I discovered my thumpy music stretched.

Stretchy, thumpy music.

It made Bob Dylan sound like a trumpeting elephant on tranquilizers; or rather, a drunken, trumpeting, Bihari elephant on tranquilizers. I was almost tempted to give him a call and play a sample: 'Hey, Bob. This is what you sound like in India.' Except I didn't have a telephone. Of course, optimists might reason you get more for your money, but lovers of classical music want to hear Beethovan's Fifth, not his Fifth and a Half.

While the television didn't produce thumpy or stretchy pictures the continual voltage fluctuations caused its silicon chip to keep going off in search of fresh stations.

'We haven't got a television,' said George sadly like a small boy. He was watching me trying to lock it into a station. We had time to kill. We were waiting, then, for the next player to enter our game of Indian Roulette and have a shot at fixing the malignant air-conditioning.

'I'm not sure I've got a television, either,' I said. Suddenly, out of the blue, via some distant satellite, we were watching Robin Leach obsequiously interviewing a fading star in his million dollar retreat.

'Wow!' George exclaimed. 'Is that how everyone in America lives?'

His astonished reaction made me wonder how Indians living in distant, rural communities were reacting to the satellite invasion. I had been told that even the most remote villages now possessed a communal set and satellite dish. For these innocent folk watching Madonna gyrate in her latest MTV video or Donahue interviewing a transvestite with five o'clock shadow and wearing a spandex mini-skirt, the only recognizable factor would be the human form and even that was of a different skin tone and speaking in an alien tongue.

It reminded me of a story I had been told in a Russian restaurant in Helsinki. During some of the Soviet Union's most repressive years a group of Latvians had escaped in a boat. The first land they touched in the West was a small island in the Baltic owned by a Danish pornographer, the Prince of Porn. With his considerable wealth he had created a material paradise; or, more precisely, a libidinous playpen. Tentatively, the Latvians inspected the millionaire's home. Huge, erotic paintings decorated the walls. Sexually explicit photographs lay scattered everywhere. The television was as big as a cinema screen and as they explored further they discovered a small cinema, too. Some of the many other appliances they vaguely recognized but they had passed through a futuristic transformation. Finally, they reached the master bedroom: black walls, mirrored ceiling, a circular bed and an open cabinet crammed with whips, chains and leather. This they assumed was a typical Western home. The 'Western World' that satellite broadcasters like STAR currently present to their newly liberated audiences is often equally as odd and untypical.

Along with the stereo and television we also bought an oven and a fridge. The oven looked the part but wouldn't play the part. When I tested it out it got hotter on the outside than inside.

'See, in the factories no one understands what they are making,' was George's explanation for the phenomenon. I immediately recalled the German tourist's comment, whom I had briefly met in my hotel bar, that while many people could speak English they didn't necessarily know what all the words meant. But George's remark was well founded. Late twentieth century gadgets, appliances and instruments are indeed being manufactured by people who work and live in nineteenth century conditions. They cannot afford and may not even comprehend the end result. This time and reality gap between producer and product gives rise to a situation where man is not yet happy with the machine and vice versa. No wonder Indian Roulette has so many players.

Other critics blame the *chalta hai* (It will do) mentality for why Indian durables don't work and why, as a result, India's consumer revolution is more a case of products revolting against their new and unsuspecting owners. Whatever the reason or cause I almost expected when the refrigerator arrived that it would get cooler on the outside than inside. Also, between purchase and delivery it had changed colour. I had picked a conventional white one. What appeared was a sickly green. Day-glo bile.

'This is not the colour I ordered,' I told the delivery man.

'No, sir,' he agreed.

'So why have you brought me a different one?'

'This colour more modern, sir.'

'Modern?' I could tell Indian reason was about to do combat with Western logic. It was a conflict, I knew, I would never win. So I accepted the Kermit-coloured fridge—better than no fridge at all, I reasoned—and since I was living under the assumption I was about to leave the hotel and move in I set off to fill it with a few basics.

There are a limited number of Western style supermarkets in Delhi and at first glance they look like the real thing with aisles and check-outs. However, on a closer inspection the items on sale are what you might expect to find in a Russian 7-Eleven: endless packages of mysterious brown bits and piles of discoloured cans. And even if you find what you are looking for there is no guarantee you'll ever get to the contents without first breaking a nail, tooth or window. In India you can find a box even Pandora couldn't open or the notorious plastic water bottle cap that thinks it's Excalibur. In fact, MY BATTLE WITH BOTTLED WATER would have been an apt title for my time in India. Indian packaging offers the ultimate challenge; a battle of mind, wits and strength over matter. Furthermore, any accompanying instructions should not be taken too seriously. They were simply included to tease an enquiring mind. PULL TAB, and the tab breaks off in your hand. TEAR HERE, and you can be sure the pack will tear somewhere else. PIERCE HOLE, but you'll need a tool kit or dynamite to do so. TURN TO OPEN, and watch your face turn red in the subsequent, hopeless encounter. These must be some of the world's first consumer products that don't want to be consumed.

*

I had watched Bill Clinton move into his White House and seen a nation celebrate. My White House received its new occupant with about as much ceremony and affection as a mugging, and to show who was boss it put the lift out of order. George and I were forced to stagger up the concrete steps with my fifteen bags and cases as water cascaded down the walls and exposed electric cables sizzled. With possessions and possessor at last united in the living room George suddenly and reverently announced: 'God bless your new home, sir.'

'Let's hope He can trump whoever cursed it,' I replied sombrously.

Although the air-conditioning was no longer under repair much of the cold air was disappearing out of the faulty french windows, and there was still a large black scar on the ceiling thanks to the conflagrant chandelier. In an attempt to cheer the place up and give it a sense of occupation I put on some stretchy, thumpy music. THE BEST OF ELASTICATED ELVIS.

'Well, at least the furniture has been delivered,' I said trying to be positive. There was a jack-sized bed—a less royal version of the queen-size I had ordered—with the standard, rock-hard coir mattress. Only, it had been put in the spare bedroom. The rest: armchairs and sofa, dining table and chairs had been arranged in the living area like a stage set. TONIGHT CHILLI SAHIB WILL BE PERFORMING HIS VERSION OF THE IMPORTANCE OF BEING EARNEST.

I told George I needed a shower and then we would go out and buy a bottle of champagne to give the occasion some pomp. On entering the *en suite* bathroom (despite my bed being in another room) I discovered it had been painted the colour of mud. Again, my orders had been idiosyncratically interpreted. 'Sahara Sun' was the colour I had selected on the paint chart; a sort of smoggy, golden glow found hanging around over Los Angeles. But urban smog had become rural mud and as I stripped, crouched before a shower head designed for or by a dwarf, I discovered water had become dust. Weird. Water had been running down the stairwell wall in a seemingly perpetual deluge. Yet another, and in this case frustrating contradiction.

I had been informed, and had certainly read every day in the newspapers, that during the eternal summer water was always in short supply. If and when it did come out of the tap it contained an unpleasant melody of viruses, microbes, bacteria, flouride and enough lime to slake a wall rather than a thirst. Apparently, under its influence toothbrush heads became punk and human heads bald. This heavy water could also, reputedly, transform a white shirt into a grey rag during a single wash. To make it lighter and potentially potable people turned their kitchens into small laboratories. These modern day alchemists vainly boiled, strained and filtered away the impurities in a desperate attempt to produce a basic, natural element.

At my company's suggestion an Aquaguard filter had been installed in the kitchen while I was waiting to move in. This was a standard gadget with a rather curious difference because whenever you turned it on it played, 'We Wish You a Merry Christmas', 'Jingle Bells', or, 'Santa Claus is Coming to Town.'

In the middle of summer, a further contradiction.

But without any water the Aquaguard was about as much use as a push bike would be to a fish.

Unwashed, unhinged, I set off with George to buy bubbly. As we shot out of the gates of what I'd already started calling the Hell

House he asked: 'You sure you want to buy champagne, sir. Be easier to find some beer.'

I'd tried domestic beer. While not all brands are as strong as Thunderbolt they all possess a vague taste of formaldehyde. Drunk in excess they create the kind of hangover that never really disappears. That may be why one brand of beer in Bangalore carries the stern warning: DRINKING THIS CAN RUIN YOUR LIFE, YOUR FAMILY AND YOUR COUNTRY. Nor is Indian wine anything to write home about. The two leading brands, Bosca and Riveria (they sound like an Italian hit team), have only experienced a brief affair with the grape and the resulting, screw-capped wrath is an effective way of embalming yourself while still alive. Indian champagne, on the other hand, is very drinkable.

But I had never tried to buy any from a store. Nor, I suspect, had George. Like everything else it involved a hunt. The only stores with the necessary alcohol licence are called English Wine and Beer Shops. What makes them English is unclear. They don't have a thatched roof, fly the Union Jack or employ cheerful cockneys. Nor do they sell anything brewed, fermented or distilled in that soggy isle. These outlets could equally be called Brazilian or Albanian Wine and Beer Shops if the only purpose was to pass the blame on to another country. Or, perhaps, they are yet another imperial relic like white lines on the road. The majority certainly resemble relics: black holes in the wall supporting a very limited selection and a long line of unshaven dependents.

Another anomaly. Although called Wine and Beer Shops they invariably don't stock either. Their patrons demand fast relief in the form of domestic rum or whisky. We had to visit four shops before finding a dust covered bottle of champagne.

'Do you have a cold bottle?' I asked.

'This only bottle,' came the curt reply.

George said something to him in Hindi and he grudgingly rubbed off some of the dust.

'Four hundred and fifty rupees,' said the shop assistant. About US $15.

George looked stunned but then in his terms I was squandering the equivalent of two weeks rent on a dusty bottle of hot, fizzy, grape juice.

'I don't drink, sir,' George declared as we were driving back home.

'You shouldn't. You're the driver.'

'Even off duty. I don't drink. It stops my brain working.'

'Yeah, I know.' I reckoned after all the recent torments my brain deserved a holiday.

*

In our absence the White House had been busy preparing its next malicious greeting. I returned to find a large group of noisy men unloading a truckload of scrap wood right below my bedroom window. At first I tried to ignore their presence, sipping warm champagne and turning the stretchy, thumpy music up to disco level. But the banging and yells still permeated through and eventually I stormed downstairs.

There appeared to be no purpose or source for all this wood. The White House was a solid concrete structure with concrete floors, walls and staircases. A multi-storey bunker. I summoned the men over. None, I quickly realized, could speak English. Then the non-swimming lifeguard appeared. I asked him where all the wood had come from.

'Trees,' he replied without a trace of humour.

'Yes, I'm aware that wood comes from trees, but what is it doing here and why am I being disturbed at ten in the evening?'

Everyone grinned and laughed as though I had cracked a highly amusing joke. In fact, what was about to crack was my temper. I should have known better. In the East if you lose your temper people will just smile and turn away. It is all to do with the complicated issue of face. I found myself screaming at the empty night but at least I assumed I had stopped them banging. Not so. Ten minutes later they resumed louder than ever. Midnight came and despite my threats to call the police they continued regardless. At two o'clock I piled some cushions on the living room floor, took a sleeping pill and eventually fell asleep in a foetal position.

I dreamed I was on an idyllic, tropical beach. White sand. Palm trees gently swaying in the breeze. Deserted. Paradise. I stepped into the warm, clear ocean and swam away from the land. I was

about half a mile out when the weather suddenly changed. Blue sky became black clouds. The calm sea turned choppy and grey. I could feel a current pulling me further out to sea. Then a solitary character appeared on the beach and I desperately waved for his attention. Finally seeing me he waved back. Against the rising wind I yelled, 'Help! Help! I'm drowning.' I experienced a brief close-up. It was the White House lifeguard, smiling, waving back like I was a friend leaving on a train.

I think I was still yelling 'Help!' when I woke up. While I had slept, and dreamed, at least another truckload of wood had arrived and the banging, which probably woke me, was worse than ever. It was also incredibly hot. The air-conditioning had failed once again and when I dragged my drugged body into the shower there was still no water.

It was time for a holiday, for all of me and not just my brain.

Immediately I arrived at work I asked Vikki to book me a ticket to Goa. 'Don't even worry about making it a return,' I added.

Corruption in High Places

GOTTA GO TO GOA I wrote large on a fax to my Indian partner in Bombay, and then George drove me to the airport at an uncharacteristic speed as if keen to be rid of me.

'You'll like Goa, sir,' he said. 'It's full of Christians.'

'I'm not going on a pilgrimage,' I replied. 'I simply need a break from the horrors of the White House.'

We came to a halt at an intersection. He pushed a hand through his angry hair. 'Me and the family haven't had a holiday for years,' he moaned.

'You can have one while I'm away.'

Being the monsoon season Goa wasn't full of Christians or anyone else when I arrived. I felt like the only tourist in town and it was a feeling I relished for almost a week. My hotel overlooked a beach which was disturbingly similar to the one I had visited in my dream. Fortunately, a string of red flags warned against swimming. Unfortunately, the hotel had a facsimile machine and just as I was starting to unwind an unusually decisive fax arrived from my Indian partner: BE IN BOMBAY BY BREAKFAST.

*

I like Bombay. It's a real city whereas Delhi is political suburb. Bombay is cosmopolitan, energetic and self-possessed. The true gateway to Asia. Our office there seemed to run more smoothly than our operation in Delhi. Most of the clients actually behaved in a professional manner. For example, some of them even paid their bills.

I had been brought to Bombay to meet a potential client operating out of an old jail. Although the building had been converted into offices a sense of incarcerated doom still lingered.

The chairman of the company, despite having invited us for a meeting, on being told we were waiting declined to see us. Instead, we were handed an audio cassette of his thoughts and shown into a heavily panelled boardroom, perhaps once the governor's office. This was one cassette that did not stretch—his dull monologue could have done with a frivolous element—although it did thump, and creak, with corporate rhetoric. For close to an hour we listened to his voice drone on and on. He was a master of the art of repetition, king of the non sequitur and a sultan of the obvious. Insomniacs would have killed for this material. One phrase I remember in particular, which he repeated several times, was that he wanted an advertising campaign that would 'outlive history'.

His own company's history was decidedly chequered. It had started as a trading company privately owned by an English family. Subsequent diversifications, including an Indian takeover, had added a basket of unrelated activities: from deep sea tuna fishing to the manufacture of three-wheeled auto-rickshaws. To positively symbolize this random diversity, as well as meet the chairman's immortal expectations, I chose a pyramid. A week later we returned to the jail to present a finished campaign.

This time he met us in person. He was a small, neat man and spent the first part of our presentation assiduously penning a thank you letter to a government minister. Only when I stood up to present did he start paying attention.

'Excuse me, Mr Curly,' he interrupted as I held up the first advertisement, 'but I must inform you that the pyramid has been used before.'

I was taken aback. I had asked around the office and no one had said they'd seen the idea done before. 'By whom, sir?' I enquired.

He looked imperiously around the room before answering. Then he said: 'The Egyptians.'

Years before, in Kuala Lumpur, I had presented a campaign to the state airline. One of my lines was: THE GOLDEN HEART OF THE ORIENT. Research had shown that many foreigners did not know exactly were Malaysia was on the map nor that it was composed of two separate territories, so the line was partly to position it geographically and also to reinforce its hospitality angle, for which the airline had a deserved reputation. Again, as I read out the line I had been interrupted by one of the dignitaries present.

'Sir, I'm afraid your line has been used elsewhere,' he declared.

'Really? With respect we checked it out thoroughly across the world,' I defended.

'So, sir, are you calling me a liar?'

'Not at all, but I'd be interested to know who used it before.'

'Oxford, England.'

'Oxford?'

'Yes, sir.' He pumped up his chest. 'I went to Oxford.'

I felt like replying: 'What, for the day?' Instead I asked why Oxford would want to call itself the golden heart of the Orient.

'So, sir, you are calling me a liar,' he retorted.

I shook my head. 'It's just that I can't understand why Oxford would make such a claim. It's thousands of miles away from the Orient.'

'That, sir, I cannot answer but at least we have established the line has been used before.'

Had we?

I left the Bombay jail equally as confused and took a taxi to the airport. Rain was pelting down, turning streets into rivers and jamming the traffic to a standstill. My driver kept making diversions and repeatedly asked what time my flight left. Every time I told him he tut-tutted, gave his horn a long blast in exasperation and turned into another back street. We arrived at the terminal with minutes to spare.

The only check-in open was surrounded by an angry mob. Pushing my way through I handed over my ticket.

'Delhi?' the clerk queried.

'Yes, but I'm very late.'

He smiled. My tardiness was obviously not a problem. A second later I discovered why. 'Sir, I'm afraid your flight has been indefinitely postponed due to technical reasons.'

What that normally meant, I'd been told by frequent flyers, was that the plane had been cannibalized due to the chronic shortage of spare parts.

'Just how long is "indefinitely"?' I asked the check-in clerk.

'I'm sorry?'

With the crowd behind me growing ever more rowdy I had to shout to be heard. 'You said the flight has been indefinitely postponed. Where I come from that means cancelled.'

For a moment he stared at me as if where I came from was another galaxy. 'No, no, sir. Flight is delayed not cancelled . . . for technical reasons.'

'I see. And what precisely are these reasons?'

'Technical ones.'

Before I became totally tied up in Indian Rope I took sanctuary in the V.V.I.P. lounge. Being a foreigner I was already considered a V.I.P., and I reckoned the inexplicable delay granted me a further superlative. V.V.I.Ps, or Double Verys, are primarily conceited dignitaries such as ministers, heads of different states, departmental chiefs, ex-prime ministers and military big wigs; residents of Powerland and modern day Moghuls. Throughout India, but not always beyond, Double Verys are treated like deity. They are the Bee's Knees, the Cat's Whiskers, the Elephant's Elbows and all those around scrape, bow and fawn, exchanging their pride for certain favours and financial 'blessings'.

Becoming a Double Very is not cheap. A seat in parliament, for instance, can cost around four million rupees. Once in power that money has to be recovered and more subsequently made. Hence the need for 'blessings'; which sometimes, allegedly, can reach the very top.

Harshed Mehta was one of the more vocal and controversial architects of the 1992 Bombay Stock Exchange scam. To a considerable furore he subsequently pleaded that he had been obliged to give the prime minister one crore (US $300,000) in a suitcase in order to 'swell his campaign funds'. Cynics reasoned that the leader didn't come so cheap. Others argued that Mehta was simply trying to generate sympathy for his forthcoming trial. If nothing else this incident gave rise to the jocular suggestion that Prime Minister Rao had started living out of a suitcase.

Ved was a Double Very of a different sort, though I would later realize he had woven a web of favouritism around many of his interests. Ved was even larger than George, my driver, and was surrounded by a group of obsequious peons as he waddled into the V.V.I.P. lounge, dressed in a tight safari suit, about twenty minutes after I had taken a seat. Waving away his supporters he immediately introduced himself in a very proper, Noel Cowardly English accent and asked if I wanted a drink.

'Thank you, but unfortunately there's no bar in here,' I replied. Besides about twenty chairs and a few dreary magazines there was little else to entertain the delayed dignitary.

'Dear boy,' he beamed. 'I ensure that fortification is always on hand.' He snapped his fingers and a peon came rushing to attend him. 'Two glasses. Fill them both half full of water.' He noticed my concern and added: 'Bottled water.'

'That's very kind,' I thanked him having hoped for something stronger than water. He nodded back. 'Are you flying to Delhi?' I asked.

'Indeed,' he replied.

'So how long do you think the flight will be delayed?'

'I would imagine now that I'm here not too long.'

I had heard stories of how Double Verys tend to use the domestic airlines like a private jet; delaying take-offs to suit their convenience, forcing less important passengers to give up their seats, even on a few occasions modifying the route to match their itinerary. But the few Double Verys I had met at Delhi's Powerland parties were aloof and puffed up with their own self-importance. Ved was puffed up but in no way aloof. I became curious as to what he did for a living.

The peon returned with the two glasses along with a senior airport official who beamed and bowed and brought over a table. 'Everyone treats you like royalty,' I said.

'They all want to know what I know,' he replied enigmatically. He opened his briefcase and, without me seeing with what, filled the glasses to the brim. 'Now this is a rather excellent whisky,' he said passing me a glass.

I took a sip. It was.

'Tell me, please. Where do you think it comes from?'

I took a second sip. Scotland seemed the obvious answer and I said so, adding that it tasted like a single malt.

'A single malt, yes. Scotland, no.' He revealed the bottle. It was Indian.

'Is this one of your companies?' I asked still prying.

He smiled back at me over the rim of his glass. 'Let us just say I have an interest.'

'So, er, Ved, what exactly do you do for a living?

'I arrange opportunities,' he replied with another smile.

Before I could enquire any further about what kind of opportunities he arranged the unctuous airport official returned to tell us our flight was ready for boarding. For the record 'indefinite', if Ved is around, is less than an hour.

We both passed through Security as Double Verys should—by bypassing it altogether. Nor did we have to join the normal boarding line. Everyone else was on board. As we sat down in business class, which is as good as it gets on Indian Airlines, the cabin crew flocked to assist Ved. This was a first. On the flight to Goa the cabin crew gave the impression they had been tortured prior to boarding and would be tortured again if they so much as tried a smile.

There was another delay before we left the dock during which Ved ordered a fresh batch of glasses, water and ice. These, once filled with whisky, he passed to the other select passengers in the executive cabin who generously toasted his health. Another first. Not only were the cabin crew smiling on an I.A. flight, so were the passengers. Had I not seen one of the attendants less than discreetly cross herself as we took off I would probably have been smiling too.

Our plane reached cruising height and Ved came and sat next to me, or tried to sit next to me. His enormity meant he had to remove the dividing arm rest and take up half of my seat as well as his own.

'So, you're in advertising,' he said after studying the business card I had given him earlier.

'Well, I was when I left the States.'

He chuckled. 'Perhaps we could do some business together.' He tapped my card against his glass. 'I would rather like this excellent whisky to be advertised in the Middle East.'

'Could be a problem,' I said.

'How so?'

'They're Muslims.'

'STAR TV is received in the Middle East, am I not correct?'

I nodded.

'And liquor advertising is permitted on this station, no?'

Again I nodded.

'No problem, then,' he said.

'So you're looking for a TV commercial?'

'I'm not so sure about a commercial. They always seem so short. I was thinking more along the lines of sponsoring a game show. Something like THE PRICE IS RIGHT.'

'A game show? I think you'll find that STAR won't let you sponsor your own programmes.'

'A mere technicality. Where there's a will, my friend, there's a way.' He took a sip then placed his hand gently on my wrist. 'Of course, if I give you this business I will expect a modest consideration in return.'

'A consideration?'

'A token of your esteem, you understand?'

At that point all I understood was that I was sitting next to a fat oxymoron: a bloated businessman who expected to be paid for getting me to do his work. 'I'm intrigued,' I finally responded. 'If we pay you for handling your business how are we supposed to make a profit?'

'Profit! Dear boy, you don't want to declare a profit in this country. You'll be taxed out of existence.'

'I mean profit in the looser sense. How are we supposed to make any money out of your proposal?'

'You'll discover, if you spend long enough here, that who you know can be far more rewarding than what you make. Scratch my back and I'll scratch yours. Am I making sense?'

'No, well, sort of.'

He refilled our glasses. By now I'd had four or five shots. Nothing was making much sense anymore.

'Let me tell you a parable to illustrate my point,' he offered. 'A poor farmer visited a junior civil servant in the nearest town to secure a permit. The civil servant asked him for five hundred rupees to speed up the process. "Five hundred rupees!" gasped the farmer. "That's more than I earn in a month." Given the farmer's circumstances the civil servant agreed to reduce the sum to one hundred. "Even this amount I cannot afford," the farmer insisted. So the civil servant suggested a payment of fifty rupees. "I came with no money. Without permit I cannot make money," the farmer pleaded. But the civil servant was determined to receive some immediate gain from the transaction. He pulled back the neck of his shirt and told the farmer to come closer. "See that bite on my back? Scratch it for me."'

'It's an interesting tale. Is it for corruption or against it?'

'Dear boy,' he responded, 'is the zebra a black animal with white stripes or a white animal with black stripes?'

He was losing me fast. 'What has a zebra got to do with corruption?'

'It's a matter of interpretation. In your country you offer a tip if the service has been performed to your satisfaction. Am I not correct?'

'Sure.'

'Well, here we prefer to tip beforehand to ensure the service is performed to our satisfaction.' He downed the contents of his glass. 'It's the cost of doing business. You have to speculate in order to accumulate.'

'But in the West we only tip people like waiters and taxi drivers. We don't tip ministers, bureaucrats and police inspectors,' I pointed out.

'Maybe you should.'

Our debate was put on hold while the still smiling attendant served dinner. Ved waved his away like it was an annoying insect but studied mine with a scientist's interest. 'May I suggest you leave the food and eat the napkin. It is without doubt far more nutritious.'

'Vegetarian, too,' I added.

Shortly afterwards he left me to play with my food and after refilling another passenger's glass squeezed in next to him. Backs and bites, I'm sure, were soon being mutually scratched.

I didn't talk to Ved again on the flight. Bigger prey had caught his fancy. But as I walked out of Delhi airport, where another group of fans had assembled to greet him, he said: 'Think my offer over. In the meantime if there's anything I can do to help, and I mean anything, just give me a call.'

*

Almost twenty years ago the journalist James Cameron wrote: 'Corruption in India is almost as leaden a cliché as hunger, it is sanctified by the oldest of traditions; it is denied by nobody, indeed the totality and pervasiveness of Indian corruption is almost a matter of national pride; just as India's droughts are the driest, her famines the most cruel, her population the most uncontrollable, so are all aspects of Indian corruption and bribery the most wholly widespread and spectacular.' And a few paragraphs later he added: 'It is ordained that every official can be bribed, every commodity can be adulterated, every scarcity can be exploited, every contract can be fiddled, every privilege can be bought, every examination can be wrangled, every bureaucrat must be paid not just to expedite the application form but specifically not to obstruct it. It is almost as though the whole concept of public morality had been gear shifted into another dimension, with another norm.'

I suspected Ved moved in another dimension and operated on another norm. My suspicions were confirmed when I showed his business card to one of my colleagues at work. 'Where did you meet him?' he asked suitably impressed.

'At the V.V.I.P. lounge in Bombay airport. We flew up to Delhi together. What's he do for a living?' His card offered no clues.

'He's a fixer. Big time.'

'What does he fix?'

'Deals. Troublesome people. Whatever.'

He sounded like an Indian don, perhaps even *the* Indian don. I tried to review our conversation to see if I had said anything untoward but it was veiled under a mist of whisky. 'He told me he arranged opportunities,' I remembered him saying.

'He could arrange a world war if he wanted to,' said my colleague still in awe.

Fixers in Ved's league move in the highest circles but to cope with the daily corruption and hassles many individuals, companies and even embassies resort to employing the services of a more modest fixer. In my company the office manager, Krishnan, doubled as our fixer. Being a Southerner his disposition was mild and reserved and no match against the tenacious, local Punjabis. Rather than fixing a situation he inevitably ended up in a fix. In fact, fixing a grin was one of his few notable achievements.

Every Monday he would give me my weekly cash allowance: a wad of holed and tattered hundred rupee notes stapled together like a book. On one occasion as I signed the receipt which, for some reason, was called a SUSPENSE VOUCHER, I asked him what was the Hindi word for 'corruption.'

'Corruption?' he echoed like he had never come across the word.

'Yes, corruption.'

He scratched his head and softly repeated the word several times in English before finding a suitable translation: '*Bhrashtachar*.'

'*Bhrash . . . ta . . . char*?'

He nodded. 'But not me. I'm not corrupt,' he quickly added.

'I'm sure you're not,' I reassured him. 'Surely, though, as a company we must occasionally pay the odd bribe to get something done?'

'No. We pay nobody,' he answered categorically.' And that included anyone who sent us an invoice.

Hanging On

From a fat man on a plane I next met a thin man who wanted a plane. Hari Dhoop was waiting for me in the Delhi office's reception when I appeared one morning breathless, having failed to muster the courage to use the vertiginous lift and instead climbed the thirteen flights. He had no appointment and I discovered he had picked our agency through a very eccentric selection process.

'I believe in the power of numbers,' he mysteriously revealed once we were sitting in the conference room, which besides being a storage area also served as the general manager's office. 'This is the eleventh day of the month. I was born on the eleventh day of the eleventh month. My only child was also born in the eleventh month. I have just purchased an apartment on the eleventh floor of a building.' He glanced at his watch. 'And, very auspiciously, the time is now almost eleven minutes past eleven. So you can see, gentlemen, eleven is my lucky number. Therefore I looked for an advertising agency with a name containing eleven letters.'

Normally, we tried to win new business through creativity, our marketing skills and by understanding the client's needs. Never had we, or I elsewhere, won an account as a result of having the right number of letters in our company's name.

Mr Dhoop wanted to start an airline. Everyone was starting an airline now that the skies had been opened up and the monopoly of Indian Airlines challenged. Some were surviving, others had gone bust.

'I have some very influential backers in Europe,' he told us, though he declined to elaborate. 'And what I will be offering is India's first domestic airline with international standards. My pilots will be European. My flight attendants Malaysian. The food will be world class. Wine, also. I even intend to provide my business class passengers with a limousine service to take them to and from the airport.'

'How many planes will you be operating?' I asked. I naturally expected him to answer 'eleven.'

'That is still under negotiation. I want to secure the very latest aircraft. You don't begin a new airline with old aeroplanes.'

'And where will you be flying to?' one of my colleagues enquired.

'We are currently examining viable routes and schedules,' he vaguely replied.

He was starting to sound like one of our typical clients.

'Seems like you have a lot of work still to do,' I pointed out.

'Believe me, things will happen fast.'

Knowing what I did of India I found it very hard to believe. 'Do you live in India?' I had to ask.

'No. London. I'm an N.R.I.'

A Non Realistic Indian, I wrote on my pad.

'So, how can we help you?' my general manager asked.

'Initially, gentlemen, I would like a delightful logo. I need something to put on my stationery and business cards.'

'Do you have a name . . . for your airline?' one of us asked.

'Feel free to give me some suggestions.'

'What a shame Virgin has already been used,' I said trying not to sound too cynical.

'Do you know Richard Branson?' he asked.

No, I don't.'

'A very good friend of mine,' Mr Dhoop proudly revealed. He looked around the room as if expecting congratulations for his name drop. I doubt, however, that any of my colleagues had ever heard of Branson.

Although we didn't share Richard's friendship Mr Dhoop and I did have a couple of things in common: a British passport and a residence in the White House. That was where he had just bought his eleventh floor apartment. It was, I already knew but he had yet to discover, sitting three storeys above the legal eight. Ironic. I had moved into the White House to find clients. Now I had found a client who was moving into the White House. But then was he a genuine client? I had my doubts. An airline with no name, no planes, no routes and probably no staff didn't sound too promising.

*

During my absence in Goa and Bombay Krishnan had played a few more rounds of Roulette and managed to get the air-conditioning working again. I also had running water. It came out of the taps the colour of weak tea and after taking a shower my hair felt and looked as angry as George's. Still it was liquid, just, and posed a quantum challenge for the Aquaguard filter in the kitchen. Cool air and heavy water. All I needed now to complete my return to civilization was a telephone.

'You should be having a phone in two years,' Krishnan casually informed me as I was trying to conceive of a name for Hari Dhoop's airline. He appeared jubilant that he had managed to cut the normal ten year waiting period down to two.

'Two years? I won't be here in two years!'

'You can have phone sooner but it won't work,' he offered.

'What?'

'Instrument, phone instrument, I can get, maybe next week. Line takes two years,' he explained.

Perhaps there are those who like to rehearse their telephone manners for two years but I was not one of them. I suggested paying someone a small consideration. I had learned at least one lesson from Ved.

'A bribe?' he looked alarmed.

'Whatever it takes,' I confirmed. 'I need a phone. Please.'

In 1986, in Delhi, 150,000 people were waiting for a telephone line. Six years later that figure had almost doubled. This was how the chairman of the telephone company summed up the deteriorating situation: 'These six years have seen alround improvement, particularly in the sphere of customer satisfaction, by way of reduction of fault rates and increasing call success rate. A big improvement has been started to bring in new work ethos. We do not claim that MTNL (the telephone company) has done wonders but we wish the facts are before you and we feel something for which the facts are before you and we feel we are on the right track and are trying harder.' Hardly reassuring to know this man is in charge of the capital's most vital communication system.

His idiosyncratic comments introduced the Delhi telephone directory. The two, thick volumes were sitting outside my apartment when I returned from work one evening even though I had yet to acquire a phone. Read the book first, I guess, was the logic. Actually, from Aakash to Zutshi it's not a bad read since it contains a bevy of useful tips and hints, some verging on the metaphysical. These appear at the top of every page in both Hindi and English and in italics to accentuate their profundity. You may consider that SPEAK INTO THE MOUTHPIECE is stating the unnecessary and I thought so too, until one night, stranded in Nagpur airport, I watched a fervent gentleman using the handset like a walkie-talkie. He yelled down the ear piece, said 'Over' and then held the mouthpiece to his ear and waited for a response. This went on for at least ten minutes.

Another hint suggests: BE BRIEF ON TELEPHONE YOU MAY BE WANTED BY OTHERS. This sounds like a tip-off: 'Hurry! Hurry! Armed dacoits are about to burst through your back door!' On a more philosophical level consider: TELEPHONE OUT OF ORDER? DIAL 198. Trying to make a call on a dead phone is an enormous mental conundrum. Equally perplexing is the advice: CHECK YOUR ADDRESS ON BILL. If it was the wrong address how could you have received a bill? But then pondering these great imponderables is one way of killing time while waiting for the phone to be fixed or reconnected after not paying the bill because it was sent to a different address; or, in my case, while waiting for the phone to be installed.

The Delhi telephone directory is also a Who's Who for name-droppers. Despite India's understandable paranoia about security the directory lists the personal work and home numbers of every member of parliament, including the prime minister, along with their home address. In the event of a life-threatening emergency, assuming I couldn't get hold of Ved, I made a note of the prime minister's home number: 301 5550.

The office manager informed me one Friday morning as we travelled up together in the sociopathic lift that he had reluctantly done 'the needful' and I should have a phone by the evening.

'Well done,' I congratulated him. 'How did you manage to get hold of it?'

'From a man who lives above you. I gave him rupees five thousand,' he replied, conspiratorially lowering his voice.

Another neighbour had obviously moved in. 'Really? He works for the telephone company?' I assumed.

'No.'

'Ah. So how's he going to get me a line?'

'He's going to give you his.'

Even in India this was not a practical solution. From the moment the phone was installed it started ringing, for him. And it kept ringing for much of the night and subsequent weekend.

'Phone works okay?' Krishnan enquired the following Monday.

'Phone works virtually nonstop,' I replied. 'But all the calls are for the man who previously had the line.'

'I see. Not good,' he agreed.

'Also, I have no idea what my number is. That makes it very difficult for anyone to call me.'

'Same number as his.'

'Yes, but what is that number?' I persisted.

While he was finding out, late one evening after far too many glasses of Bosca wine—the domestic embalming fluid—I made my phone call to the Prime Minister. In lieu of a national emergency I decided instead that I was going to ask him whether he had ever noticed how the shape of nan bread resembled the map of India. Was this a coincidence or some clever, patriotic ploy? If it was the latter I was going to patent an American shaped hamburger and subsequently a whole range of jingoistic junk foods.

These are the kind of thoughts an abundance of Bosca provokes.

Unfortunately, I was unable to put this question to the Indian chief. Although I let the phone ring for several minutes it was never answered. Even if he had gone out on a wild Thunderbolt binge I would have expected a secretary or servant to take the call. Perhaps, like thousands of others, his phone wasn't working. Or perhaps my call had been diverted to some distant place like Bhoom, Tonk or Zero.

'Less than a quarter of calls dialled get through to the right

party,' I was told by a friend at one of the diplomatic missions. 'It's much better than it used to be, though. A few years back a senior minister stormed into his local exchange waving a loaded revolver because he could never get a call through.'

But my, and the senior minister's, phone problems were nothing compared with those of an indefatigable gentleman by the name of Dinesh Chaparia. In 1992 he was awarded a consumer prize for living with a dead phone for thirteen years. He also holds the record for the maximum number of complaints lodged without any result since 1977. Remarkably, he still pays his telephone rental charges in the vain hope that his phone will one day come to life. When my own phone died, still without me knowing its number, it was like the Unknown Soldier or an unidentifiable corpse. Requiems have been composed around lesser subjects.

*

'What's wrong with your company's phones? I've been trying to call you for days,' Hari Dhoop yelled down the telephone line about a month after we'd first met. We had eight lines but seven were permanently engaged, even when the office was empty. I also had a 'private' line on my desk. A red phone. The Hot Line. But whenever I picked it up there was always a heated conversation in Hindi going on.

'Apparently, it's the exchange,' I tried to explain. 'It's overloaded.'

'Give them a bribe. Only way in India,' he continued to yell even though for once the line was crystal clear.

We agreed to meet for lunch so that I could show him a selection of names and logos. The venue he suggested was a psuedo-Japanese restaurant in Connaught Place. What made it psuedo was that all the food on offer was Indo-Chinese, which filled me with dread after my earlier piscine encounter.

'I must warn you,' he said after ordering two sweet lime sodas, 'that your company has severe cash flow problems.'

'What gives you that impression?' I asked with as much interest as I could muster.

'Last week I was in Madras. It was rather embarrassing, I can assure you. For some reason the hotel I was staying at would not accept my American Express Gold card. So I called on your office there and asked for a 40,000 rupee loan. They said they didn't have the money.'

Wise people, I thought. Having an account at an advertising agency was not supposed to be the same as having one at a bank. 'Well, they probably didn't know who you were,' I suggested.

'I explained I was one of your clients. Made absolutely no difference.'

'I'll take the matter up with my Indian partner,' I said knowing I wouldn't.

'We share another mutual interest which is causing me some concern,' he went on.

'And what's that?'

'The White House. It seems my apartment there shouldn't exist. They have violated some building regulation. This I luckily discovered before paying the rest of the purchase price. Now I have to get my deposit back. Never easy in this city.'

'I'm sorry to hear that,' I said, wishing my own apartment there didn't exist. 'Anyway, on a more cheerful note, would you like to see some of the names and logos we've come up with for your airline? '

'Ah yes, the name.' He glanced briefly at the menu. 'You see, I've been thinking, and I'm sure you've come up with some very clever ones, but I have decided to call it Baron Airway.' He paused to judge my reaction. My only reaction was that many man hours had been wasted looking through the dictionary. 'If you count the letters . . .,' he added.

I already had. 'Eleven,' I said. 'But I wish you'd told us you had chosen a name. It would have saved us a lot of work. It also means that none of the logos are appropriate.'

'I'm very sorry. I tried to tell you but your telephones are never working.' He still wanted a reaction. 'What do you think of Baron Airway?'

I didn't think much of it. 'Why Baron?'

'It exudes a romantic power, as in press baron. And the initials are the same as British Airways,' he replied.

'It could be confused with "barren", as in arid or infertile,' I pointed out.

'Given the quality of my service I think that is unlikely,' he countered. 'Flying with us should be a very fruitful experience.'

'So you have some planes now?' I assumed.

He picked up his lime soda and took a contemplative sip. 'Let us say that I'm very close to signing the agreement.'

'I see.' I also took a sip. This was like playing poker without any cards. 'So I suppose, since you've picked a new name, you'll be needing another logo?'

'I would be exceedingly grateful. Time is ever pressing. Something baronic.'

We finished our lunch which he either lacked the funds or the will to pay for, and as we were walking out of the restaurant he enquired whether I knew anything about computers.

'I know my way around them reasonably well. Why?'

'They're the future of India,' he said. 'I'm thinking of starting a computer company here. Baron Computers, why not?'

An airline, a computer company, if he diversified any further I could probably sell him a second-hand pyramid.

Having been through the exercise once we didn't try too hard designing his logo the second time round. With a little adjustment Fresh Air—our inspired, and no doubt controversial, suggestion for an airline that on paper, at least, had offered such a different approach—became Baron Airway, and what was once light blue became ultramarine (eleven letters). A few days later he called me again.

'You really must get your phone lines seen to. I thought you chaps were supposed to be in the communications business.' Attack was patently his first line of defence. Once I had muttered an insincere apology his tone of voice changed. 'I've been trying to get through to enquire whether you enjoy the company of pretty women?'

'Well, yes, naturally.' I paused. 'What's the catch?'

'Catch? You misunderstand. Three beautiful Malaysian ladies are currently parading in front of me wearing my new uniforms. I would appreciate your informed view on the subject.'

When I arrived at this office—a small ground floor apartment in central Delhi—he was right about the women's beauty but the uniforms looked like something worn in a factory producing hazardous chemicals.

'What do you think?' he asked. The women spun round like

models. 'My good wife designed the uniform.'

'Very original. Perhaps a shade conservative, though. After all, you're trying to win the hearts of businessmen.'

'This is not Europe. One must appreciate the moral climate in this country. Not a good idea to reveal too much flesh,' he cautioned. Compared with his uniform a wet suit wold have been more revealing. He dismissed the girls and ushered me to sit down. 'I must be honest with you,' he said. 'My plan to lease a fleet of brand new planes was, I fear, a shade ambitious. But I do now have one confirmed.'

'Only one?' A one-plane airline sounded about as hard to sell as a pair of trousers with only one leg, but then he had named his company 'Airway' rather than the conventional 'Airways.'

'From small acorns . . .' he alluded.

'Where's the plane coming from?'

'The King of Bhutan, a personal friend, is kindly lending me one,' he replied. 'And I was thinking your clever boys could come up with a transfer.'

'A transfer?'

'No point repainting his plane. We could stick my logo over his. Of course it is important the transfer stays on when the plane takes off.'

'Of course,' I could only agree. 'Where exactly will this plane be taking off from . . . and flying to?'

'The inaugural flight will be from Delhi to Madras. However, I have one small technical problem to overcome.'

'Lack of spare parts,' I said with a grin.

He looked bemused. 'Spare parts?'

'It's just an old Indian Airlines joke,' I tried to explain. 'So what's your small problem?'

'Regrettably, I've come up against an unforeseeable hurdle regarding my finance package. Nothing serious. Only a temporary snag. Should be resolved in a week or two.' He thoughtfully ran a finger down the tail fin of a model plane standing on his desk. Baron Airway had been crudely written on the fuselage. Then he asked, suddenly more cheerful: 'Oh, by the way, did you bring my new logo with you?'

Foreign Exchange

At least twice George had remarked as we drove 'home' through the gates of the White House: 'This place always looks half-built, sir.'

I wasn't sure if it was half-built or half-falling down. The evidence could have pointed in either direction. The lobby had remained a building site, sizzling ropes of electrical cable continued to dangle dangerously in the stairwell, the health club was still unhealthily empty and the lift, when it worked, was invariably full of dusty builders clutching planks of wood. Closer to home a massive spike of voltage had terminally fried the air-conditioning, the Aquaguard filter had given up trying to tame the wild water and the rains had flooded the communal satellite dish. Madonna no longer provocatively danced for me. The BBC failed to inform me. Even Robin Leach was unable to offer me caviar dreams, or whatever it is he peddles. When an environment collapses the occupant has a clear-cut choice: move out or go insane. For some strange, unaccountable reason I chose the latter.

With no phone, either, and with only the arid lifeguard around who could speak English I felt possessing a rudimentary knowledge of Hindi might prove prudent. Learn the language and everyone becomes your friend and the country becomes a home. However, never a natural linguist, I immediately had a problem with my nasals, plosives and liquid aspirates. For Westerners getting the pronunciation right, I decided, required a heavy head cold or a detached larynx, or, ideally, both. There was another problem. No one seemed too sure how many vowels and consonants there were in the language. According to the first book I'd bought, LEARN HINDI IN A MONTH, there were eleven vowels (had Hari Dhoop edited the book?) and thirty-three consonants, but a second book on the subject, UNIVERSAL HINDI TEACHER, told me Hindi consisted of sixteen vowels and thirty-six consonants. Since the second book was approved by the Ministry of Education and endorsed by the President I was tempted to go with this version. On paper all the consonants and vowels looked identical, anyway. Besides, all I needed were a few useful phrases.

Phrases used in language books never seem to have much relevance to day-to-day situations and I've always wondered what kind of lives the writers of these books lead. They're forever catching trains, demanding to see a doctor, haggling over the price of vegetables and asking for directions. At least the writers of my two Hindi books lived slightly more imaginative lives. They did things that involved questions and statements like: 'Show me the tongue,' 'Count my clothes,' 'Do not fire,' 'How much is wanting?' 'Can you see me?' 'Damn it! What is there in this village?' and, 'Cool reasoning is different from agitated opinion of the moment.' All well and good, but what I needed were pert, succinct translations for questions like: 'Why does it take six months to repair my air-conditioning?' I also needed the ability to understand the replies.

One of the books told me, 'There are two genders in Hindi. *Pulling* = masculine. *Striling* = feminine.' Striling? Perhaps the author meant striking, as in what a strikingly beautiful woman. It was late, about eleven o'clock, as my mind wandered off into a land of secret saris and the even more secret French lingerie that was supposedly worn underneath, but before it could wander too far it was wrenched back into reality by a sudden explosion of hammering and drilling. I rushed out to see what was happening. Through the adjacent apartment's open door I saw a platoon of near naked men demolishing, 'pulling' down one of the central and possibly load-bearing walls.

'Shut up!' I yelled. 'It's very late. Shut up!'

Absolutely no response. I could have been invisible. Maybe I should have tried the phrase 'Can you see me?' in Hindi. Instead, abandoning cool reason for agitated opinion of the moment, I stormed back into my own apartment, grabbed one of the Hindi books and urgently searched for an appropriate phrase.

'*Chup raho*!' I tried screaming at them. ('Be quiet!')

This time they briefly acknowledged me with a smile and a hand flick, but not my request. Like men possessed they continued with their demolition. Equally as possessed I stormed downstairs to confront the management. The lobby and the management office was as deserted as a moonscape. Even the lifeguard was not around. The only person I could find was a sleeping guard who I knew could not understand English. I dashed back upstairs for my Hindi book, yelled again at the workmen, then returned to wake him up. He jumped out of his seat as if he had seen a ghost—a ghost reading a book. It took me several minutes to find even one applicable phrase or word during which he stood patiently at attention.

'*Dusri man: zil,*' I finally recited. According to the book this meant 'first floor'. I was unsure how to handle the colon.

He looked at me blankly.

'*Dusri man: zil,*' I repeated pointing to the floor in question.

He nodded back but not in comprehension as I ransacked the book for another suitable word. '*Aadmi,*' I suddenly found ('Man'). There was no plural listed so I said it several times.

'*Aadmi? Aadmi?*' he vaguely repeated.

We were making progress. If only I could find the Hindi for banging. In the search I came across the word for ten. There were about ten men working upstairs. '*Das aadmi,*' I said to keep the conversation alive.

'*Das aadmi?*'

'*Ha! Ha!*' I was trying to say 'yes', not laughing. But I could tell he was growing increasingly uneasy about this mad European shouting gibberish at him from a book. I gave up trying to find 'banging' and used 'elephant' instead. Big animal making lots of noise was my deranged rationale. '*Das hathi aadmi dusri man: zil,*' I concluded. ('Ten elephant man first floor.')

His eyes widened as be backed away.

'Bang! Bang! Bang!' I desperately added.

'Bang? Bang?' he mouthed.

At which point the 'ten elephant man' appeared out of the entrance. As they walked past one of them said to me in perfect English: 'Good night.'

*

This was my book buying phase. Books do furnish a room and my rooms needed all the help they could get. So did I. From trying, and

ENGLISH
HINDI

so far failing, to master the language I was determined to learn more about the country. Compared with the West books are inexpensive in India and I would return with encyclopaedic armfuls; instant paper friends, some more eccentric than others.

Most of the eccentrics had been brought together in the LIMCA BOOK OF WORLD RECORDS, India's own version of the Guinness Book of World Records. Whereas Guinnesss is black, creamy and alcoholic, Limca is green, fizzy and non-alcoholic, though a shot of gin or vodka can give it a purpose. And the only purpose, it seemed, behind the feats contained within this thick book was to elevate the performer above the grim anonymity of Indian life. Why else would a man spend four years writing a 7,872 foot long letter on the subject of World Peace? And yet another painstakingly inscribe 4,160 letters on a single grain of rice? Some did absolutely nothing but wait, like Kalyan Sain who grew his moustache to a width of 10.72 feet, and like Swami Maujgil who stood still for seventeen years. More actively, Arvind Pandey took 107 days to run the distance between Los Angeles and New York, and he did it running backwards; while Jagdish Chandra took fifteen months to crawl nearly a thousand miles. To celebrate their extraordinary efforts V. Jayaram broke the world record for applauding nonstop: a total of over 500,000 claps. Compared with theirs my own trial of endurance with the White House was hardly record breaking; though it was, I realized one morning as I stared into the mirror, rapidly pushing me towards a breakdown.

COPING WITH INDIA should have contained at least ten volumes. Instead, it was a rather thin paperback written more for the traveller passing through than the long term resident passing out. It appeared no book had yet been written for the latter.

'You should write a book about your experiences here,' one of the booksellers suggested. Over the months we had become good friends and he frequently recommended an eclectic title to add to my library. Such as CURIOSA SEXUALIS, which if nothing else had cheered my mood with its bizarre tales. One recorded how a woman had changed sex simply by jumping over a ditch. Unfortunately, A CABINET OF UNUSUAL ILLUSTRATIONS, listed in the contents, had not been included in the Indian reprint.

'Write a book?' I answered. 'Such is my current atrophy that I can't even fill out a form.'

Then I discovered HOBSON JOBSON; a glossary of hybrid, Anglo-Indian words and phrases compiled by two Victorian gentlemen, Yule and Burnell. Leaving aside the Delhi telephone directory this proved to be one of my best reads—a delightful potpourri of philological curios. Many of the words possessed an onomatopoeic quality you could almost taste. This was the language I had been looking for. Forget 'Show me your tongue,' or 'Count my clothes'. Forget, even, 'Cool reasoning is different from agitated opinion of the moment.' Instead, I could from henceforth utter profanities like: CHOPPER COP! KUDD! GRUNTH! and SEA CUNNY! And it didn't matter a jot if no-one understood what I was saying, including myself. I now had my own collection of mantras, as well as a string of expletives cunningly veiled as Raj Hinglish. It was, if I recall correctly, shortly after this discovery that the first firework went off in my mind.

The second, more a fiesta, went off in the middle of the night several days later when the mysterious woodmen returned. Previously there had only been one truck. Now there were two and at least twice the men and ten times the noise. To combat their banging I turned up my stretchy, thumpy music as loud as it would go. With the marble floor and bare walls it was amplified still further but not enough to black out the banging. When I threw open the door to charge downstairs I found the woman who always ran away from me, and one of the few other tenants, standing there looking absolutely terrified, the music pounding behind us.

'Poggling budzats!' I cursed in my new language. In one movement the woman turned and fled to the safety of her own apartment.

On reaching the outside yard I discovered the men had erected a pile of wood the size of a pyramid; their attempt to outlive history. In the moonlight it took on a ritualistic presence. 'Kudds! Bhoots! Bheels!' I insanely yelled as I pulled planks from the pile and hurled them back on the truck. Above me Pink Floyd's WALL was being stretched to its thumpy limit.

The security guard briefly appeared but on witnessing my manic state backed hurriedly away into the shadows. Transcending language and reason I grabbed another plank of wood and chucked it through the manager's plate glass office window. He had promised there would be no more deliveries. He had broken that promise, so I had broken his window. Native logic.

My demented act of vandalism stopped the men in their tracks. Jumping on to their trucks they drove out of the compound as if under attack. I returned to my apartment, switched off the music and felt strangely at peace with the world. Little did I realize as I climbed into bed that the manager's idea of revenge would be to try and kill me.

Night Life?

I was woken very early the following morning by a loud banging on the door. It was my agency's general manager looking hot and anxious. 'What happened here last night?' he demanded to know, his voice several octaves higher than normal.

I told him I had finally had enough of wood being dumped outside my apartment and taken the matter into my own hands.

'Not a good idea,' he said. 'Why didn't you phone the police or me?'

'The phone doesn't work,' I reminded him.

'This man is a very dangerous man,' he said referring to the Bihari manager. 'He's a gangster. A real gangster. He summoned me here this morning. It was not a request. Just now he told me if you were an Indian you'd be dead. Because you are a foreigner he will take his time. Believe me, he means what he says. We must get you out of here and fast.'

I began packing my fifteen bags and cases.

'Just take the essentials. We can send someone back later for the rest,' the general manager urged.

We walked to my car where George was nervously waiting. A gang of the manager's well-built bodyguards looked on waiting for the slightest provocation. Even the lifeguard turned away from me.

The entire incident had left George bemused. He had heard from the guard how I'd been drunk, crazed and shouting strange words as I threw chunks of wood across the lobby and finally one through the manager's office window.

'It's the stress,' I told him as we drove out of the White House compound never to return.

'Stress?' A possible illness seemed to cheer him up. 'I suffer from stress, too, sir.'

'Really?' I should have known.

'Yes, sir. It affects my legs. Makes them ache. It's because I sit down so much driving. All the stress runs into my legs.'

I wanted to change the subject. 'It's the heat, also. I've never lived anywhere so hot. It's relentless. In God's name, when does it start getting colder?'

'Christmas,' he flatly replied, disappointed that I wouldn't discuss his latest ailment.

I was moved into the sanctuary of another five-star hotel. This one overlooked the Delhi Golf Club. I had a room with a pastoral view, a telephone that worked, nonstop air-conditioning and a television full of satellite programmes. A reassuring cocoon of civilization. I also had an important soccer match to watch. England were playing Norway. Unfortunately, it was being broadcasted not by satellite but by Doordarshan—the national, state-run network. Roughly translated the station's name means 'Seeing what is far'. The match was being played in London but from the poor quality of the transmission it looked like it was being played on Pluto. I had prepared for the game by giving room service an extensive order. A DO NOT DISTURB sign had been placed on the door and all incoming calls blocked. Lying on my queen-sized bed, sipping Kingfisher beer—Thunderbolt's milder relative—I was in tip top shape to enjoy one of football's most anticipated matches. But the local broadcasters had a few unpleasant surprises in store. The first occurred as a coordinated attack was being launched on the Norwegian goal. At a critical moment the game was interrupted by a very long commercial break. When we returned, several minutes later, all the players were at the other end of the pitch.

Worse was still to come, however.

At full time the score was a draw. Extra time followed and both teams added another goal. It was still a draw. Time for a penalty shoot-out. Each team matched penalty for penalty. Then Norway missed. If England could score victory would be ours. But as the player ran to take the kick the screen went blank. There was a long pause followed by the caption: TODAY IN PARLIAMENT. India might wait ten years for a telephone to be installed but it won't wait ten seconds for a penalty.

*

I ended up watching so much television, or reading books, because there's not much else to do in Delhi once the sun has set. That ubiquitous, catch-all Indian phrase for events beyond one's control 'What to do?' could well have been coined to describe the capital's night life. Bombay provides its night owls with tasty morsels, some more decadent than others. Bangalore is famous for its pubs, Calcutta for its coffee houses. In these and other major cities people enjoy the night but in Delhi they seem afraid of it. Come dusk and a voluntary curfew descends. Once the last bus has trundled home at the early hour of ten the streets become disturbingly deserted, especially in New Delhi. The only rare pedestrians are those forced to walk or guard. Even cars disappear as if hired just for daylight use. Those few that do appear scuttle from place to place as though on a secret mission.

When I first arrived I had suspected a conspiracy. I was convinced that a vast, subterranean and Bacchanalian network of clubs, bars, casinos and discos existed. All I had to do was ask the right person. So I began asking. I asked the people who worked for me: 'Where are some of the fun places to go in Delhi?'

'Fun? In Delhi?' they responded guardedly. Who was this sybarite?

'Well, what do you do in the evening?' I persisted.

'Go home.'

To be fair some of them lived miles away and by the time they reached home it was probably time to leave for work again. But others lived closer. What did they do after they got home?

'We mainly watch STAR TV. Sometimes we have friends or family around.'

'When friends come round do you have a party?' I asked hoping for an invitation.

'No. We watch STAR TV.'

Nor was the concierge at my first hotel of much help. He told me there used to be a disco in the hotel but it was closed down due to inter-caste violence. 'Some of our guests go jogging at night. It's quite safe,' he added without much enthusiasm.

'In this heat?'

'There's a cinema in Vasant Vihar that shows quite recent American films. Or you could rent a video. We could put a player in your room,' he suggested.

I ended up renting a video. It was the *Addam's Family*. At least that's what the title said on the cassette. It was a pirate copy shot in a cinema on a handycam. I've been to the movies in the States hundreds of times but never seen an Indian pointing a video camera at the screen. Whoever was responsible for filming the *Addam's Family* had a problem keeping the camera still. Maybe he had simply fallen asleep. Anyway, I saw more of the audience than the film and the dialogue was barely audible under the munching of popcorn, slurps of soda and laughter. Also, earlier than the director had planned, the film came to an abrupt conclusion. I guess the pirate had run out of tape, or been thrown out of the cinema.

Being British I decided to visit the British High Commission to see what they could offer their marooned citizens in the way of entertainment. Even an amateur rendition of Gilbert and Sullivan or a few Scottish flings would be better than nothing. However, after a short interview with the Community Liaison Officer it seemed I would have to make do with nothing.

'Summer is always dead in Delhi. Most of us take our home leave,' she revealed.

'So winter is livelier?' I assumed.

'No, not really. Most diplomats spend a lot of time at official functions. Quite frankly we all rather enjoy a quiet evening at home.'

Watching STAR TV, no doubt.

'But is there a club at the mission I could join?'

'You need to be proposed and seconded by people working here,' she said. 'And there's a long waiting list.'

'I don't know anyone here,' I said.

'Some of our younger staff go running. The Hash House Harriers on Monday nights. It's a good way to meet them.'

Jogging? Running?

Besides, I'd come across the Hash House Harriers before, in Hong Kong and Kuala Lumpur where they originated. Basically, it was the unspeakable in pursuit of the undrinkable; a horde of perspiring, podgy expatriates shouting 'On! On!' as they crashed through the urban countryside trying to find the next clue on their way to a finale of warm beer and fraternal insults.

While at the High Commission I decided to register my name

just in case I had to be suddenly air-lifted out. In the waiting room was a fellow countryman attempting to renew his passport. His port-veined face suggested he knew where to have a good time.

He laughed. 'I'll tell you, my friend, before I came here I was working on a North Sea oil rig. It was like Las Vegas compared to this bloody place.'

'So what do you do in the evening?'

'Stay at home and wait for power cuts,' he confided.

I began to wonder whether everyone stayed at home because there was no night life, or was there no night life because everyone stayed at home? I received an answer in the TIMES OF INDIA one morning. According to a study it had commissioned the majority of Delhi's middle class didn't even watch television or entertain friends in the evening. They said they didn't have time. They preferred to work! I could only further wonder why none of these workaholics had applied for a job with my company.

'I tell you,' I told one of my more pleasure-seeking and comparatively industrious creative colleagues, 'If Debbie had decided to do Delhi instead of Dallas she would probably still be a virgin.'

'Debbie?' He looked baffled, even slightly disgusted by my frank revelation. 'Is she a girlfriend of yours?'

'What? Heavens no! It's the title of a famous American porno movie: *Debbie Does Dallas*,' I explained.

'I see,' he said, though I wasn't sure he did. Later he came up to me and, as if playing a game of NAME THAT MOVIE, suggested another title in the 'Does' series. 'Given that you're always sick and complaining how hard it is to do business here, how about: *Delhi Does Kelly*?' he said with a grin.

If nothing else he had given me an alternative title for this book.

*

It was with a mixture of anticipation and scepticism that I accepted an invitation from a group of expatriates to join them on a ribald evening visiting one of Delhi's few hot spots, notwithstanding that during summer every spot is hot.

'We're all meeting in the bar at the Imperial Hotel first,' I was told by Henry, an Irish engineer down for the weekend from a chemical plant in Punjab.

Somehow, I cannot now remember precisely how or why, Gosh—the superfast-talking art director—came along with me. There were a dozen of us in the bar of the Imperial. After several rounds of beers 'the jokes began telling themselves' as Henry put it. One I can still recall. It concerned a Sardarji—a conservative Sikh—who came home after being away for two years and found his wife with a baby. He was furious and accused her of being unfaithful. 'Me, unfaithful? But I could never love another man,' she protested. 'So how did you become pregnant?' her husband demanded to know. 'Every night I slept with a photograph of you,' she amorously cooed. Her husband accepted the explanation but the following evening he returned home angrier than ever. 'Woman, I do not believe your story,' he yelled. 'That photograph is only of my face!'

Gosh also told a joke. Under the influence of alcohol he achieved the extraordinary feat of being able to speak even faster. A monotonic exchange of rapid word fire. The joke he told should probably have lasted at least ten minutes. Instead, 'Lone Ranger . . . naked blonde . . . posse not pussy,' was condensed, like an advertisement, into thirty seconds.

'You speak too fast,' someone told him.

'I think even faster,' he replied with a loud cackle.

From the Imperial we drove in convoy to the Blue Star Café, 'the naughtiest club in town,' according to Henry.

'Not a good place to visit,' George cautioned when I told him where we were going.

'Why?' I asked.

'Women there not nice.'

Gosh shot off several rounds in Hindi and roared with laughter when he had finished.

'Did you understand anything he just said?' I asked George.

'No, sir. He speaks in code.'

The Blue Star Café was little more than a shack with an incongruous, giant cement cup and saucer standing guard outside. A weather-beaten sign promised: CABARETS. We each paid one hundred and fifty rupees and were presented with a strip of leather like a book mark.

'What's this?' I said.

'Buffet,' answered the cashier.

'Buffet?'

'Exchange inside for food,' he explained. 'Eat a lot. Thank you.'

Inside were about a hundred men surrounding a catwalk. To one side there were three steaming cauldrons which constituted the buffet.

'Please enjoy,' a waiter told us as he waved away several squadrons of flies from the food. We all to a man declined his offer and ordered beer. 'No beer. Soft drinks only,' he said.

Fortified with Thunderbolt, or even Kingfisher, the place and the show might have been bearable but with our alcoholic investment at the Imperial rapidly wearing off, it was not. The twelve of us sat on a long wooden bench like patients in a doctor's waiting room while the rest of the audience regarded us with understandable suspicion; or, if they already knew the tame content of the show, amusement. Then the lights dimmed, a green spotlight flooded the stage and the band began to play—rather, began to practice.

The first girl looked like George in drag, although if anything she was even larger. Ved in drag. Covered from head to toe in a hundred veils she began prancing around the stage but not in time to the music since it lacked any recognizable tempo. When the band finally ran out of notes she stormed off still fully clothed. A minute later she reappeared amongst the audience and began shaking everyone's hand.

'Why did she shake our hands?' I asked Gosh. I wished I could have asked someone else.

'Strangers . . . friends . . . fuck,' he yelled merrily over a fresh attack of music.

'Why?' Henry queried, unable to catch Gosh's reply.

'Strangers . . . friends . . . fuck,' I repeated.

Henry shook his head. He was none the wiser, nor was I.

Several more girls followed, in various shapes and sizes, and each on completing her 'cabaret' came and shook our hands. We were like visiting royalty watching an ethnic dance. It was all too much, or too little, for Henry.

'Aren't the girls ever going to take their clothes off?' he bellowed at a waiter over the din of the band.

'You want chicken?' the waiter yelled back.

We stayed for about an hour during which not one stitch of clothing was removed. As we filed out Gosh indicated he would be staying. 'Later . . . plenty . . . wow!' he promised, but when I saw him at work the following morning he looked decidedly unrewarded.

I drove back to my hotel for a nightcap with a foreign correspondent. He had been working in India for nearly five years and knew some of the ropes if not all of them.

'For a country which was once so open on matters sexual it's hard to understand why the subject is now taboo,' he began. I could see George straining to listen. 'I wrote a piece some three years back. Do you know that most men only visit a brothel because they've never seen a woman naked?'

'You mean young, single men,' I assumed.

'No, not at all. About four fifths of married men have never seen their wives naked,' he corrected. 'This society has become very sexually repressed. Most men are unaware that women are capable of having an orgasm, so are most women. Even the language has been puritanized. What we call sexual harassment they call "Eve teasing". Supposed to make the offence less shocking, I guess.'

'God is punishing sinners with AIDS,' George evangelically chipped in, unable to restrain himself any longer.

'Ignorance is punishing people with AIDS, more like it,' said the correspondent. 'At a recent doctors' conference I attended over half of those present had next to no idea about the disease, despite the fact that there are already more than a million carriers. By the end of the century there will be at least fifteen million victims.'

'We volunteered our services,' I said, 'and I produced an extensive campaign. We even got most of the media for free but the appropriate authorities weren't interested.'

'The government won't take the initiative, just the funds. Here's a deadly communicable disease but the government is unable, or unwilling, to communicate the dangers because anything to do with sex cannot be discussed openly.'

The following morning while driving me to work George nervously asked: 'You can't get AIDS by talking about it, can you, sir?'

*

Not long after my visit to the Blue Star Café one of my international clients flew in. I'd first met him while living in Hong Kong and had spent several nights showing him the town. With Delhi it was going to be a short show. As we sat having drinks in his hotel he wanted to know what nocturnal pleasures I had planned for him.

'Well,' I said, 'I thought I'd buy you dinner here and then, because you're probably pretty jet-lagged, perhaps an early night.'

He looked disappointed. 'That doesn't sound like too much fun. Besides, I'm not jet-lagged. I've only come from Singapore. So where's the action?'

'There's not a great deal of action here to be honest,' I had to admit.

'Really? Capital city. Nine million people. Land of the Kama Sutra. There must be some place where everyone goes in the wee hours?'

'Yes, there is. In fact thousands gather there from all over the world. And there's loads of cheap Western wine, liquor and beer.'

'Great,' he said rubbing his hands together. 'What's it called?'

'Indira Gandhi International Airport.'

The Art of War

When the British ruled India from the heights of Simla they would, during moments of tepid boredom, play the strange game of 'Ye Shepard's Race'. This involved forming pairs (always a popular pastime), going up to a tethered sheep and singing: 'Baba, black sheep have you any wool?' Understandably terrified, the sheep would plaintively bleat back. The couple then had to write down what they thought the sheep had said.

I read this account in two books and both concluded by saying that the first couple to arrive at the correct answer won the prize. Correct answer? Was the competition being judged by another, wiser sheep? Even during my blackest moments in the White House I had never resorted to trying to guess what animals were saying.

Today, Simla, as it is now called, is the capital of Himachal Pradesh, one of India's most beautiful states. I travelled there out of season to play Ye Account Race. We'd had the Himachal Pradesh Tourism account for several years, I was told, but it had been forgotten like buried treasure. Since the Director of Tourism had changed three times no one ever stayed in office long enough to remind us. Now the incumbent wanted a campaign.

I sent a fax to my Indian partner in Bombay: 'I've just discovered we have the Himachal Pradesh Tourism account and that it's about to go up for review with a number of agencies. Please send reinforcements.'

No fax returned but Mani Pillai arrived from Madras.

From the moment we met I could tell he wanted to be a politician. The handshake, the poise and the repetitive name-dropping. He had been at school, it seemed, with every senior minister and had been a 'personal friend of Rajiv Gandhi'. He wore thick, black plastic rimmed glasses with lenses so powerful that they magnified his eyes into oysters. Balding, he kept his hair long at the back. And he was always chuckling as he planned his next madcap scheme.

'For the past five years I have been working on an economic model that will revolutionize the way this country works,' he proudly told me after I had accepted his invitation to buy me lunch.

'I thought you worked for our agency in Madras?'

'Yes, I do that also,' he reluctantly admitted.

We went for lunch on the top floor of a central hotel overlooking a smoggy Delhi. The amoebae had returned, or clones had, and my stomach had been left behind in the express lift. I excused myself and went in search of the nearest toilet, but when I later tried to open the cubicle door it was stuck. Although I howled for ten minutes or more I knew I was beyond shouting distance from the restaurant. So I began kicking the door and eventually succeeded in knocking it off its hinges. Windows. Now doors. I was becoming a professional vandal.

I had been gone for at least thirty minutes but Mani was still studying the menu. He looked unconcerned when I returned.

'I locked myself in the loo,' I explained.

'Why?'

That shouldn't have been his response.

But then Mani never responded according to convention. Over lunch he managed to avoid answering nearly all my questions—an old political trick—preferring instead to tell me in massive detail about his plan for a new language which would unite the country.

'English, you see, has too many negative associations. The Raj and all that. And now American imperialism. What I'm working on is something like Shaw's Esperanto. Based on Sanskrit. Hindi belongs to the *Hindu*. My language, which I've yet to give a name, will belong to everyone.'

After a long lunch with Mani, made even longer by my imprisonment, I felt I knew his views on everything except how to retain the Himachal business.

'Shouldn't we be concentrating on the business at hand?' I suggested as we drove back to the agency.

'Himachal? Don't worry about that. Easy job. Just sell it like it was Switzerland, only without the clocks and the efficiency.' Before I could respond he added, 'Listen. Can I borrow your car for the afternoon? I have a very important meeting lined up with a minister who's interested in my economic plan.'

Mani, much to George's chagrin and my annoyance, made a habit of borrowing my car during his stay in Delhi. As a result I was always waiting for him to return or employing Um's services if his car was available. I suggested he did the obvious and used Um, but he seemed less than keen on the idea.

'This Mr Mani from Madras is a strange person,' George mentioned as we returned to the hotel one evening.

I wasn't sure George should be discussing a senior member of the organization's management in such a critical manner but curiosity got the better of me. 'Strange in what way?'

'He talks to himself, sir. At first I though he was talking to me, but he wasn't. Just talks to himself, all the time.'

'What does he talk about?'

'A lot of it is in Tamil, so I don't know. When he speaks Hindi all he talks about is the government.'

Over another lengthy lunch Mani said: 'You don't appear to have too much business here. You need some more clients. Maybe I can help. Having gone to university here I have some top-notch contacts.'

While Mani was off independently pitching for new business I began working on the Himachal campaign with Gosh. I immediately dropped the 'Switzerland' angle and eventually came up with the concept of comparing the beauty and tranquility of the mountains with the hell of urban life, of which I was fast becoming an expert. The idea was to attract the middle class city dweller away for a short, recuperative break. For example, one advertisement showed an executive in a busy office tied up on several different telephone lines. In contrast we showed him at one with nature holding a fishing line. Another showed commuters crammed into a suburban train. This was compared with a couple enjoying the view on the Simla toy train. The most indulgent advertisement showed a black page with the caption: TYPICAL METRO POWER CUT. Against this we showed a couple romantically posed against the setting sun. The urban hell we portrayed in grainy black and white. The glimpses of heaven in colour.

'I like it,' Mani announced before I'd even finished showing him all the work. 'And if they don't like it we can always give it to another client. In fact, I met one this afternoon.'

The HOW! NOW! WOW! logic was threatening to return.

'I blinked they'll like it,' I said. 'And we can make it more topical when something goes wrong in the city like strikes, stock market crashes, water shortages.'

'Since the ideas are obviously flowing can you give me one for a share issue?' he asked. 'Need to show them something by tomorrow.'

'What?'

'Share issues are all the rage. Easy money. Full page advertisements in every newspaper,' he explained. 'There's a gold mining company in Assam about to go public. Should buy a few shares yourself.'

'This is a new area for me. What's the ad supposed to say?'

He blinked back. 'Why, buy some shares, of course.'

I gave him STRIKE IT RICH there and then and insisted he commenced working on his side of the Himachal presentation.

'I think I've come up with a novel approach,' he said.

'So you've already started?' I was surprised.

'I'll show you some notes tomorrow,' he promised.

When Sun Tzu wrote *The Art Of War* two and a half millennia ago he probably had no idea he was also writing Mani Pillai's presentation to the Himachal Pradesh's Department of Tourism.

'It's war in the city. That's what we're showing,' Mani pointed out after he'd revealed his novel approach: to take chunks from THE ART OF WAR and change the words accordingly. 'And we're promising through a victorious campaign—note the pun—peace in the mountains.'

'It's a very loose analogy,' was all I could think to say.

We departed for Simla two days later; me with my 'victorious campaign', Mani still plagiarizing extracts to support it. The plane we boarded was a small, flimsy twelve-seater operated by Vayudoot—a remote cousin to the national carrier, Indian Airlines. The plane climbed and climbed and, without ever really descending, landed on a plateau in the clouds. This was Simla Airport, according to a sign on the control tower, but there was no evidence of habitation for miles around.

A reception party was waiting, I assumed from the Tourist Board, and I walked over to meet them. As I drew closer I could see they were looking beyond me. I turned and saw a Double Very, a very plump Double Very waddling towards them.

'Wait here. I'll organize a taxi,' Mani instructed.

The taxi turned out to be a dilapidated Maruti van. It was supposed to seat six but nine of us climbed in.

'How far is it to the town?' I asked as we set off.

'About twenty kilometres,' I was told.

We had travelled about one of those twenty—along a winding, narrow road—when the van suddenly lurched to one side and almost fell over the edge. Everyone jumped out to discover a puncture. The problem, soon revealed, was that there was no jack. Instead, the passengers had to hold the van's side while driver and co-driver replaced the faulty wheel. The spare tyre, I noticed, was as bald and smooth as a billiard ball. Not a trace of tread to be seen.

Mani had booked us into Oberoi Clarkes, one of Simla's original hotels. Situated at one end of the Mall it reminded me of an English guest house, which is what it had once been. Time slowed down once you entered and, I suspect, without any help from valium. The hallway clock ticked, or tocked, as though it was on the verge of running out of clockwork. The staff, literally old retainers, shuffled around with their backs bent and the receptionist studied Mani's credit card like it had yet to be invented.

'Wash and brush up. Leave in ten minutes?' said Mani after we had eventually been appointed rooms.

'Look, I still don't think our presentation hangs together,' I said, making a final attempt to get him to change his approach.

'Don't worry. They won't understand a word you say, anyway.'

We had an appointment to meet the Director and his team in their offices By three o'clock. At three-thirty I was still waiting in the hotel's hallway for Mani to finish his wash and brush up. I'd tried calling his room numerous times. The line was always engaged.

'Christ, Mani!' I exclaimed when he finally appeared. 'Arriving an hour late is no way to win the business.'

'Calm down. I have been talking to my spy in the Department of Tourism. It has been agreed that the Director will come to our hotel for the presentation. At seven tonight. Always better to fight on home turf.' He gave his head a triumphant toss. For him the battle had already been won.

If we had been prudent we would have spent the remaining three hours preparing and setting-up our presentation. Mani, typically, had different plans.

'Do you want to see the highest cricket ground in the world?' he asked.

'Where is it?'

'Chail.'

'How far away is Chail?'

'About forty kilometres.'

The trip from the airport, a distance of twenty kilometres, had taken nearly two hours. Mani was now suggesting we embarked on at least an eight hour journey even though we had a presentation in less than three hours.

Another firework went off in my head.

'Sure,' I said. 'What the hell.'

Mani rented a chicken soup Ambassador from the hotel. It came with a driver who had only half decided to get into the car. He drove in a three quarters position, back wedged against the door, arm hanging out of the window. With a lot of honking we set off. We had been twisting and turning for about forty minutes when the road stopped. An avalanche had brought a deluge of boulders crashing down. There was an ancient DIVERSION sign but no alternative route.

'No money,' said Mani. 'No money to maintain the basic services. Country's falling apart.' He stared at the rubble. 'Back to the hotel, I suppose.' The car negotiated a ten point turn. 'You know,' he went on, 'during the monsoon season, in Chail, they used to play cricket in dense mist.'

My moment of revenge from the locked-in-the-loo incident had arrived. 'Why?' I asked with a victorious smirk.

*

The director and his team of one arrived close to eight. Mani had hired the hotel's conference room, once its ballroom. The four of us tried a occupy a corner. After a few pleasantries Mani stood up and announced: 'The Director and his esteemed colleague do not

DIVERSION

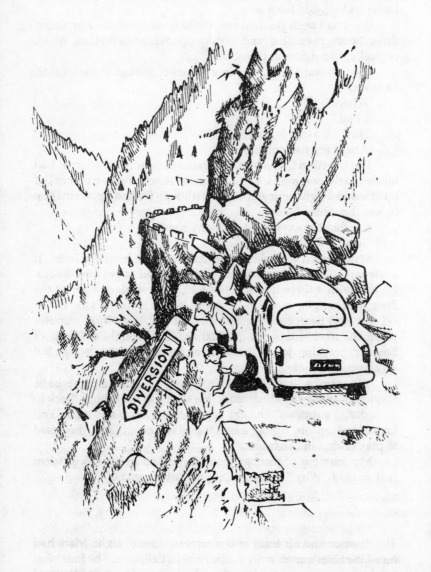

understand much English. So, if you don't mind Neil, I will present my part in Hindi.'

I have no idea how well Sun Tzu's *The Art of Advertising* translated into Hindi. When Mani finally finished presenting I couldn't tell, either, whether the two clients were enthralled or bemused.

It was my turn.

I spoke ever so slowly as I showed the work and then went on to explain it in detail and how it could expand out in the future. Both heads nodded during my speech. At the end Mani asked if there were any questions. The Director stood up.

'I did not understand part of what Mr Curry said.'

'Which part?' Mani enquired.

'The part I did not understand.'

When all else fails make 'em laugh, so I told the joke about the Sardarji and his photograph. Everyone obviously understood it because they all roared. Or perhaps they were simply being polite, humouring the unintelligible foreigner.

'That was one of the strangest presentations I've been through,' I said to Mani in the bar afterwards.

'I think it went very well.'

'Really? How can you tell?'

'They stayed until the end.' He called the geriatric waiter over. 'I think we both deserve another drink. And tomorrow I'll show you the top of the world.'

I slept intermittently that night. The mountain air was soporific. The climbing trucks, compulsively changing gears, were not. But their heavy loads brought me dreams and one was as vivid as my Goan nightmare when the waterproof lifeguard had failed to save me from drowning. In this particular dream Mani, myself and the two Himachal Pradesh clients were crammed into a cubicle, perhaps the same one which had imprisoned me in the Delhi hotel. Within this limited space I was hopelessly trying to present the advertising campaign.

'Wadjit humper expo,' I said nonsensically. Something like that. It could have been a sentence constructed out of Mani's home-spun Esperanto.

'What Mr Kettle is trying to say,' Mani translated, 'is that the photograph is only of his face.'

Mani was always late but he rose early. At the unearthly hour of six he called—yanked me out of another, unremembered reverie—and suggested we set off on our walk.

'It's incredibly early,' I protested.

'The early bird catches the worms.'

'I don't like worms.'

He laughed but remained persistent. 'See you downstairs in fifteen minutes then?'

It was barely light and for once pleasantly cold as we walked up the Mall, turned by Christchurch and began the ascent of Jakhu Hill. We passed bungalows as English as Agatha Christie with brown monkeys scampering across their corrugated roofs.

'Hanuman is the monkey god and one of the chief characters in the Ramayana,' Mani informed me as the gradient began to increase. 'Once he jumped from India to Sri Lanka in a single leap.'

'So what's his association with Simla?'

'He rested here on his way to save the life of Laxman, Ram's brother. To commemorate the occasion a temple was constructed on the summit.'

I looked up. The hill was of Himalayan proportions. Clouds covered the peak. 'We're going to climb all the way?' I gasped.

'Run if you like. I used to as a boy.' He started running, sort of running ahead.

My lungs were full of Delhi smog which together with the altitude made breathing difficult, let alone running. I followed behind at my own pace, cautiously avoiding the monkeys which increased in numbers and size as I neared their god's shrine. When I reached the top I found Mani staring out into the mist like a lost sea captain.

'The view's not what it used to be,' he remarked sadly. Burt Lancaster had once said the same thing about the Atlantic Ocean in the film *Atlantic City*.

After returning to our hotel for a much delayed breakfast Mani found out, somehow, that the Director had been impressed by our presentation and would make a decision 'within hours'. That the hours became days; that perhaps, inadvertently, we had presented to the Department of Retardation rather than the Department of Tourism seemed to concern Mani about as much as me: very little. I was enjoying the break, living out my advertisements, proving that Himachal was indeed the antidote to urban hell.

After four peaceful days in our highland retreat we expanded our horizons and took a trip on the Simla to Kalka toy train. Even by modern day standards this is an incredible feat of engineering involving a climb of 4,200 feet, 102 tunnels and 870 bridges. Keen to avoid another aerial encounter I had originally planned to travel the whole way to Kalka and then connect with the overnight express to Delhi, leaving Mani behind to await the Director's decision. But on talking to the clerk at the Simla ticket office I was informed that such a journey would not be possible.

'Why not?' I asked expecting the answer to have little relevance to my question.

'At such short notice impossible to guarantee a seat on the Delhi Express,' I was told. So we both bought a ticket to the third station down the line. A hired car, the same one which had attempted to take us to Chail, was instructed to follow us.

With time to spare before the train departed I walked down to photograph the ageing locomotive. As the shutter was closing a turbaned head bobbed up from inside the cab. 'Good morning,' it said. 'Are you a professional photographer?'

'More a keen amateur,' I replied.

The driver dismounted from the footplate and standing rigidly to attention offered me his hand. 'My name is B.S. Gill, driver of this train. I am the most famous engine driver in India.'

I shook his hand. 'Is that right? What makes you so famous?'

'I am an artist of considerable repute,' he boasted. 'My work has appeared in *India By Rail* and the magazine *Perspective*. I'm also currently enjoying an exhibition in Simla which I would be most pleased if you visited.'

'Certainly,' I agreed.

'And how far am I taking you this morning?'

'Just three stops.'

'Would you care to join me on the footplate?'

'Sure. Thank you.' I climbed up forgetting to inform Mani.

B.S. Gill introduced me to the fireman, coal black and missing most of his teeth. With a blow of the whistle we huffed and puffed out of the station.

'I was most fortunate to visit Russia several years ago,' B.S. Gill said over the roar of the engine. 'A land of splendid locomotives, some of the finest in the world. In Moscow I was shown round the engine shed by a driver called Tractor. An odd name, you will agree, and I asked him how he had acquired it. He told me that during Stalin's collectivization programme in the thirties many parents called their sons Tractor. I said would call my next son Locomotive. Locomotive Gill. My wife, however, was less than keen on the idea.'

I had dressed as if for cricket that morning, or to demonstrate the power of a bionic washing powder: white shirt and white trousers, but not for long. They were white when we steamed into the first tunnel, as sooty black as the fireman's face on coming out at the other end. B.S. Gill regarded me with a jovial roll of his eyes.

'Not the best colour to wear on the footplate,' he smiled. 'Should wash out, though.'

I dismounted at the third station looking like a cartoon man who had been left holding an exploding bomb. 'Thanks, I think,' I said.

'Don't forget to visit my exhibition,' he called back as the train steamed away.

Only two of us had alighted. An amazed Mani walked towards me like a wary gunslinger. 'Heavens!' he exclaimed. 'What's happened to you?'

'I decided to take in a little local colour.'

There was no sign of our car outside, or any other vehicle. A small group of elderly villagers turned to stare at my impersonation of a chimney-sweep with a mixture of curiosity and fear.

'So what do we do?' I asked Mani.

'Good question.' He walked over to the group and within seconds arms were pointing in every direction. 'There should be a bus coming past in about an hour,' he told me returning.

'A bus? With me looking like this?'

'Not a lot of choice, I'm afraid.' He let out an unnecessary giggle. 'You should see what you look like.'

It was almost two hours before the bus appeared and when it did it looked like it had been travelling for at least a century. We squeezed on board. On seeing me the other passengers fell silent. I felt darkly and uncomfortably conspicuous. Treacherous, also. Here was the man trying to sell their peaceful utopia to hordes of noisy urbanites.

When Mani joined me for dinner that evening he revealed that the Director had decided to award us his business. Our holiday was over. The following morning we returned to the plains, and the pollution, and the chaos. A few days later Mani rang me from Madras.

'Guess what?' he asked.

'What?'

'According to my spy the Director is about to be replaced. Everything's on hold until further notice.' And then he started giggling. He was still giggling as I gently replaced the receiver.

Looking for Lutyens

Edwin Lutyens and I seemed to have much in common. It took him twenty, frustrating years to build imperial Delhi, during which costs dramatically escalated, designs were continually changed or compromised and he finally ended up not talking to his partner, Herbert Baker, for five years after a protracted and bitter row over the inclination of the gradient rising to the Viceroy's house.

Admittedly, my partner and I were still talking but most of our communications were through epistolary faxes, and while I was not designing a capital fit for an emperor, I was finding it hard, as well as frustrating, trying to design campaigns which would fit my clients' eccentricities and mood swings. They, too, demanded endless changes and compromises. Also, throughout his stay in India Lutyens was dogged by ill health, some of if more mental than physical. 'Everything is so anxious-making here,' he wrote to his wife in England.

That was something else we had in common.

On returning from Simla to a late, autumnal Delhi I found most of the toxic pollutants had become trapped under a smoggy lid; a consequence, I was told, of weather inversions. In protest my respiratory system went into hiding. This time it wasn't just a cough I couldn't get rid of, I just couldn't breathe.

I called the British High Commission. Surely a breathless Brit deserved instant attention? I ended up talking to the same woman who had suggested I join the Hash House Harriers.

'I'm afraid our medical unit is only for those working at the mission,' she explained.

'You don't seem to offer your citizens here much in the way of assistance,' I said, predictably adding: 'It's our taxes that pay for this whole kit and caboodle.'

'We will help in the event of an emergency.' Her voice became gritty.

'Not being able to breathe is an emergency.'

She recommended a private clinic close to my hotel; a large, fifties-built home with two modern annexes attached on either end like glass arms. A row of credit card decals welcomed patients in, but inside it was as if a village had taken the building hostage; children screaming, parents yelling, blank bodies being pushed through on squeaky trolleys while the receptionist had her head in her arms and, incredibly, was fast asleep. The only other scene of tranquillity amidst this chaos was a poster for Goa. As once I had dreamed, but never experienced, the sea was crystal blue: tempting, tempting.

'Hello!' I yelled at the receptionist.

She stirred, looked up, her own dream shattered. 'Yes?'

'I'd like to see a doctor.'

'About what?'

'I'm having trouble breathing.'

'You need a chest x-ray,' she said in a flat, disinterested voice. She probably said the same thing to every new patient. All part of the initiation ceremony.

'No, I don't. I think it's some kind of reaction to the pollution,' I replied.

An hour later when I finally saw the consultant he said the same thing: 'Let's x-ray your chest.'

'My chest was x-rayed a year ago in the States. It's fine,' I told him.

'How much did it cost in the States?'

'What?'

'The x-ray. How much did it cost in the States?' he repeated.

'It was part of a general check-up. I don't know, about $100.'

'Only 300 rupees here.'

'Good value, I'm sure, but I don't need one,' I insisted.

He stared at me as if possessing x-ray vision, then countered. 'Please, if nothing else it will tell us what you haven't got.'

There was a long queue inside the radiography department and the radiographer worked without any form of protection—no doubt glowed in the dark. You were supposed to put your card at the back of the stack. I slipped mine at the front and my name was immediately called. Hostile eyes burned into me but at least I was learning to beat the system.

'Your chest is fine,' the consultant grudgingly admitted after studying my x-ray.

It took a few more visits and a few more tests before he reached the final diagnosis. I was allergic to diesel fumes.

When I told George he naturally sympathized. 'They affect me also, sir, these fumes. They fill my head with lead.' He tapped the side of his head and for a moment I expected to hear a dull metallic sound. 'My head, I keep telling the wife, is getting heavier.' He moved it from side to side. 'Heavy head.'

With a crop of angry hair on top and a pair of stressed out legs below.

'I've got to find another home,' I said to divert his attention.

'What's wrong with the hotel, sir?'

'The bill for a start. Also, I'm starting to feel like a man on the run. And I've decided I want to live in a Lutyens bungalow.'

From the moment I began seriously searching for a new home George tried to switch his role from driver to surrogate wife. He suggested what I should be eating, wearing and even offered to dye the increasing number of grey hairs my current situation was giving me. Worse, he kept picking up brokers, bringing them to meet me at work or at the hotel, and insisting I saw what they had to offer. Most turned out to be characterless boxes. One even had a trumpet learning landlord living above who keenly enquired whether I enjoyed 'jazz-like music.'

'George, I don't want a modern house or flat. I told you, I'm looking for a Lutyens bungalow,' I kept repeating. And every time we passed one I pointed it out.

'You want an *old* house,' he at last realized.

One Saturday, after another lengthy and unsuccessful search, I stopped at a hotel for lunch. Walking into the restaurant I saw Ved, the super fixer.

'Dear boy,' he bellowed. 'Please be a gentleman and join us.'

He was sitting with a man about a quarter his size. Together they looked like a ventriloquist and his dummy.

'This is Om,' Ved said. 'He's like a brother to me.'

I didn't enquire into the precise nature of their relationship. Instead, I told them about my frustrating search for a home.

'Should have given me a call,' said Ved. 'I have a marvellous house in Defence Colony. Just been completely redecorated. Five bedrooms. A palace.'

I felt my back being seductively scratched. 'That's very kind but it sounds too big.'

'You'll grow into it, I'm sure. Go take a look.'

'What I'm really looking for is an old Lutyens bungalow,' I said.

'Still a colonial at heart, eh?' laughed Ved. He tore off a slice of roti and scooped up the remains of his buffet.

'I admire his work. He's an incredible architect,' I replied in defence.

'Neil's an . . . artist . . . in advertising,' Ved, still chomping, explained to Om. He burped and gave his ample Delhi belly a fond rub. 'We met not so long ago and discussed the possibility of advertising whisky in the Middle East.'

'He's a genius,' Om suddenly declared in a voice so high he sounded like Michael Jackson. 'Whatever he suggests you should do.'

Ved lapped up the praise. 'Why don't we all have dinner tonight? My treat,' he suggested. 'And in the meantime I'll see if I can find you a suitable relic of the Raj.'

'Tonight . . . ?' I hesitated trying to think of an excuse.

'Excellent!' Ved declared. 'Call me from the lobby. Around seven? I'm staying in room 1237.'

When I called him from the lobby at around seven he told me to come upstairs.

'Welcome to my humble abode,' he greeted me. 'Help yourself to a drink.'

His room had been decorated with enough flowers to start a florists. Along with the blooms there were presentation boxes of chocolates, baskets of fruit and numerous bottles. Om was already there, or had always been there, lying on the bed watching the television.

'Is it your birthday?' I asked pointing to all the gifts.

'Every day is my birthday,' he said with a chortle.

I poured myself a whisky and sat down. 'Any luck with my house?' I tentatively asked.

'It will happen, dear boy. If not today, tomorrow,' he replied. Completely out of context he added: 'Om's in oil, you know.'

'Is he?'

'Owns refineries, ships, pipelines. Don't you?'

Om nodded. Again his mouth opened but nothing came out. The Silent Tycoon.

'So, what do you fancy eating tonight?' Ved asked.

'I'm easy. I hear there is a very good French restaurant in this hotel,' I said.

'I hate the French,' Om announced with obvious deep feeling. I waited for a reason but none came.

'How about Indian, then?' Ved mediated. 'I'll book a table.' He picked up the phone, barked something in Hindi and then became agitated before finally slamming down the receiver. 'Unacceptable! Telling me their restaurant is full,' he told us. He picked up the receiver again and dialled a string of digits. Another, more measured conversation took place. 'The situation has been happily resolved,' he said on completing the call.

I was about to witness how the truly powerful in India always get their way. Minutes later his room bell rang. It was the hotel's general manager profusely apologizing for 'the confusion' and saying that a table was now waiting, the best table in the restaurant. Naturally, to make up for the inconvenience everything was complimentary.

'Including a bottle of your finest champagne, I trust,' Ved said.

'Of course, sir.' At this point the manager would probably have given him the hotel in reconciliation.

We walked into the restaurant and were greeted like rock stars. Other guests turned their heads and looked disappointed that they didn't immediately recognize us. Our table was set apart from the rest with a bottle of champagne—French not Indian—already cooling in the ice bucket.

'The lamb is their speciality,' Ved said. 'However, Om is a vegetarian. What would you like, Om?'

Om studied the menu while an increasing number of the restaurant's staff congregated around our table. After much deliberation he selected a cauliflower dish.

'This is all very impressive,' I had to admit. 'Who did you call?'

'The chairman of this chain of hotels,' Ved revealed.

When the lamb arrived it smelled delicious and I was hungry

enough to eat a flock. But as I lifted up my first loaded fork Ved yelled: 'Don't eat it!'

'Why not? I'm starving.'

'Because, dear boy, it has been cooked incorrectly.'

Who cares, I thought. However, the entire staff of the restaurant did care. Within seconds they were earnestly grouped around Ved. During the ensuing inquisition, conducted entirely in Hindi, the chef was summoned from the kitchen and the hotel's general manager reappeared. Throughout, Om silently munched through his monochromatic cauliflower dish.

'The problem,' Ved told me after the inquisition had been completed, 'was that the lamb had been *boiled* before going into the tandoor. Quite unacceptable, dear boy. A travesty no less. So we're having chicken instead.'

Later, I would hungrily dream about that lamb.

*

Ved, perhaps, could have arranged the next world war but he appeared unable to arrange a Lutyens bungalow. In fact, I never heard from him again. It was George who finally located my dream home once I had encouraged him with a small financial inducement. He woke me one morning to break the good news. 'It's *very, very* old, sir,' he added as if that was all that mattered.

Kum Kum Bungalow had been designed by Lutyens to accommodate the court musicians who played for a nearby maharajah. It was situated at the end of a dirt track. A jhuggi surrounded two sides even though a row of small houses stood empty opposite. There was a lawn, a large kitchen garden, a hundred foot kapok tree, parrots and monkeys. It felt remote but over the garden wall I could see India Gate.

'So, sir, what do you think?' he asked after showing me around.

'I think it's splendid. Will the squatters next door be a problem?'

'If they are, sir, we can move them out.'

A bout of ethnic cleansing was not my idea of a house warming party. 'So how much is the rent?'

'I don't know, sir. You'll have to discuss that with the landlord.'

I returned the following morning to meet the landlord; a short, plump ex-diplomat who had represented India in Prague and Beijing. Now in his eighties he spent the first hour of our meeting dropping heavy names.

'Tell me about the history of Kum Kum,' I eventually suggested.

'It is a very famous house. In the fifties the King of Nepal came here to sign a treaty,' he replied.

I'd like to think the King of Nepal signed his treaty a lot quicker than we signed our lease. What should have taken a few days ended up taking weeks as the landlord kept adding new clauses to an ever ending list. He wanted a massive deposit involving the exchange of some junk bonds he had unwisely purchased, a subscription to numerous foreign periodicals, a fax machine and an imported car. (I catered to his last request by bringing a toy car back from England). And every clause he added had to be sent to his son in Washington D.C. for approval.

'You sure you really want this house?' My Indian partner asked after yet another extended meeting with the landlord. 'I'm going to end up exchanging my company for it.'

'We haven't even agreed what the rent is going to be.'

'The rent?' He laughed. 'That's a minor technicality. Let's get you into the house first.'

And so it was, with the rent still being negotiated and further clauses being debated or added, that I moved into Kum Kum. It was a beautiful morning with a clear blue sky and birds singing. As George carried my fifteen bags and cases into the house I stood in the garden and breathed in the fresh air. For once my lungs didn't reject it.

The Moonlit Mali

Kum Kum came with a mangy, black and white mongrel called Wilbur and two nameless servants who had stayed on even though the previous tenants had left three months earlier. One was a young chowkidar, the other was an old mali.

'Who has been paying their wages while the house was empty?' I asked George.

'Nobody, sir. They knew someone would eventually move in and give them back pay.'

'Back pay?' That's the landlord's problem. I want to hire my own servants. Besides, the chowkidar is always asleep.'

'He's a lazy man,' George agreed. 'I'll find you a new guard.' Before I could stop him he had left on a recruiting mission. He returned in less than an hour. 'The man I have found you is very, very ugly,' he proudly announced. 'He will frighten everyone away.'

He certainly frightened me, would have frightened Frankenstein. Kum Kum now had its own resident Freddy Kruger. But unfortunately the current chowkidar refused to quit and locked himself in the servant's quarters. I ended up with the new chowkidar guarding the old one while we attempted to resolve the situation.

'He'll have to come out eventually, sir, to eat,' George said.

'Unless he took a supply of food in there with him.'

As it turned out he had.

The mali, I discovered, only over worked during the hours of darkness. He would arrive soon after the sun had set and then spend hours crashing around the garden. After a couple of days of watching this strange behavior I called him over.

'Why do you work at night, mali?'

'Yes, madam,' he replied.

'George!' I yelled almost in panic. 'I need your help.'

George was now recruiter, house manager, translator and occasional driver. After talking to him George told me the mali worked at night because he preferred to. It hadn't worried the previous tenants.

'But how can he see what he's doing?' I persisted.

Back came the translated explanation: 'He can see very well in the dark. He's had years of practice.'

The mali was an extreme example of the German Tourist's Principle: he could speak a little English but had absolutely no idea what any of the words meant. I was always 'madam' and it was always 'Good morning' even though we only over met after dark. Sometimes he would show me the fruits, and vegetables, of his labour. Pointing at a potato he would declare: 'Big cabbage, madam.' But then he had been tending the gardens of Kum Kum for over seven years and, providing he didn't have to speak English, appeared to be a useful asset.

Once I moved in the local bush telegraph went into overdrive. Wallahs appeared offering wickerwork, carpets, quilts, wood carvings, furniture and papier-mâché abstracts, though perhaps not by design. Just as persistent were potential employees offering their services as a cook, cleaner, bearer, sweeper and, in one amalgamated case: 'I am a man of many trades, sir.'

Most servants carry a file of chits written by previous employers. These are his or her references, but sometimes they are forged; as was the case of one candidate who was sent to see me, though he could not remember by whom. According to his chit he had worked for the 'Swidish' Embassy. It began: 'He had good worked and excellent cooked. He now all the Swidish fook. He now bakery of good bread and pastrs. He making a meanue and took care guest and climbing superwisiring. Also is a come right on time duty. He bever miss on duty. I am pudishop to recemmandation and he was worked porar July 15.' His chit had been signed by the 'personil offiser.'

'You do need a cook, sir,' George pointed out. 'My cousin's sister's nephew is a very good cook. He once worked at the Ethiopian Embassy.'

'I can't hire anyone until we get the old chowkidar out of the servants' quarters,' I reminded him. 'Should we call the police?'

George looked nervously around. 'Never involve the police, sir. They're more criminal than the criminals. I'll talk to him.'

After numerous interviews I finally hired a cook who had previously worked for the Mexican Embassy. Not wishing to break up his marriage I also hired his wife as a cleaner cum dhobi. The cook, but not his wife, could speak reasonable English and I explained to him that initially he and his family, they had a small girl, would have to share a single room until the imprisoned chowkidar had released himself.

'Yes, sir. But where will my servant sleep?'

I had no idea that in India servants had servants. 'Why do you need a servant?'

'She looks after our daughter, sir.'

'Can she join you later, after we've sorted this mess out?' I requested.

'No problem, sir,' he willingly accepted.

Somehow Krishnan, the officer manager, had succeeded in getting my furniture and other fixtures out of the White House, despite a death threat still hanging over my head. Although I ended up living but a mile away from that blasted ivory tower everything arrived looking like it had been shipped half way across the world. The mattress had acquired lumps, the plate glass on the dining table had been cracked and one of the armchairs had lost a leg during its escape. But at least my stereo still played its stretchy, thumpy music, even if the oven continued getting hotter on the outside than the inside, a phenomenon that seemed to fascinate the cook for days. Things were slowly coming together but then, thanks to George, my immediate world suddenly threatened to fall apart.

'The squatters next door are getting very angry, sir,' George informed me one morning.

'Angry? Why? I've done nothing to upset them.'

'No, sir,' he agreed.

'So why are they angry?'

'They are ignorant people, sir.'

'So?'

'They pay no rent or taxes,' he continued, 'and they are tapping your electricity.' He pointed to a cable running from the side of Kum Kum and stretching over the garden wall.

'I agree that has to be stopped. I'll get Krishnan from the office to talk to the landlord. I still don't understand why they're angry.'

George looked sheepish. 'Perhaps, sir, because I told them you were going to have them removed.'

I was furious. 'You had no right to say that. Live and let live is my policy. You go and tell them that. Say you made it all up.'

'But, sir, that's a big loss of face for me,' he protested.

'It will be a big loss of job for you if you don't do it,' I warned him.

But the damage was done. Returning from work that evening there was a group of ten or more standing menacingly outside my gate. George, stupidly, repeatedly hooted them to move.

'Are you crazy? I want to pacify them not turn them into a lynch mob.'

'I'm frightened sir,' he admitted. I could tell he was.

'I thought you used to be a boxer and a soldier?'

'Used to be, sir. But my strength, it's disappeared.'

I stepped out of the car falsely smiling like a politician on a campaign trail. One of the squatters stepped forward. 'What's the problem?' I asked.

He pointed at George trying to hide behind the steering wheel. 'Your driver is throwing his weight around. We have as much right to live here as you. More. Some of us have lived here for forty years.'

'He made a mistake. He's sorry. I'm sorry,' I apologized.

'This is our country, not yours,' the spokesman concluded. He returned to his group, said something and we were allowed to pass.

That night I slept uneasily, half expecting an invasion to come pouring over the garden wall. I needed friends in India, not enemies. With first light I heard someone outside on the verandah. Gingerly pulling back the bedroom curtain I saw it was the immured chowkidar enjoying a moment of freedom. He was holding a piece of paper and quietly laughing over whatever was on it. This was my chance. I dashed through the house, threw open the back door and was stopped in my tracks by a crazed Wilbur. While I was trying to calm him the chowkidar rushed past and I heard him slamming the door of his voluntary cell.

'Almost caught him, sir,' said the other chowkidar with a wide, distorted grin.

'Why didn't you stop him?' I yelled.

'But, sir, you didn't ask me to,' he said surprised. Then he shrugged, grinned again and wandered off.

I walked round to the front of the house and found that the piece of paper which had amused the chowkidar was still lying on the floor of the verandah. I picked it up. It was an electricity bill, for Kum Kum. Had it been for millions of rupees, that might have been funny—except for the person paying it—but it was for an average amount.

At work that day I told Krishnan about my chowkidar problem. A look of weariness crossed his face. 'I'll come round this evening,' he reluctantly promised.

That evening George, the cook, the new chowkidar, the office manager and myself assembled outside the old chowkidar's room. We were a motley crew.

'I can't understand what he's living on,' I said to no one in particular.

'I'm feeding him, sir,' the cook cheerfully admitted.

'You?' I was astonished. 'We're supposed to be starving him out. He's not a guest!'

Meanwhile Krishnan had a conversation going with the inmate. George was shaking his head over what he was hearing.

'He says if he gets his back pay he'll leave,' Krishnan turned to tell me.

'How much is his back pay?'

'Rupees three thousand.'

'Okay, we'll pay him.'

The office manager scratched his need. 'But he doesn't work for us.'

'I'll pay him then.'

George came closer and tried to whisper. 'Not good, sir. If you pay him everybody will lock themselves in there.'

'Don't be ridiculous,' I reprimanded him.

'You don't understand these people,' he finally succeeded in whispering.

These people? I stared at him. Was he an android? 'George, all I understand is that I want him out of here. Offer him two thousand rupees to vanish.'

A bargain was struck. The chowkidar came out beaming and

proceeded to generously shake our hands. He looked like he had just come back from a relaxing vacation.

*

Once the chowkidar had left life at Kum Kum became comparatively normal, except for the fact that the cook could only produce Mexican food no matter what I requested. On one occasion—when I had an important, potential client coming round for dinner—I asked whether his culinary skills could stretch to something more European.

'I'll get a big fish, sir,' he said.

I laughed but he had no idea why. The reason I laughed was because seven years earlier, in Taiwan, someone had said something very similar and equally out of the blue. I had gone to Taipei to help our agency there pitch for the Moony Diaper account. According to the brief I'd been sent Moonys were unique because 'they were especially designed for the Asian baby's bottom.' Not being an expert on such matters I assumed the Asian baby's bottom was basically the same as an European's. Apparently not.

I reached Taipei about ten hours before Typhoon Wayne scored a direct hit. With my hotel—oddly called The Brothers—literally shaking from the onslaught. I tried to come up with a memorable line which could work in Mandarin. I turned the television on in the hope it might inspire me. An in-house movie was playing entitled *The Plan for Fish*. A prophecy as it turned out. I had water on the television and rain driving against the window but I was dry of ideas. After much deliberation and even more Carlsberg I came up with the slogan: MOONY DIAPERS—THE ONE BABIES SCREAM FOR.

Once the weather improved the agency came round for a presentation; not just one or two of them but virtually the entire staff of twenty, pushing and squeezing into my modest room. None, except one, could speak English and he became my translator, sort of. When I spoke for seconds he would speak for minutes and vice versa. When I said something which I thought was funny his translation didn't provoke a single laugh, yet frequently the audience chuckled away when he was translating some of my more profound points. At the end I had no idea whether my contribution had been a hit or not. Finally, the chairman of the agency whispered something to the translator who turned to me and said: 'He would like to buy you a big fish.'

The fish served to my guest and myself at kum kum was not big. I'm not sure if it was even a fish, and I tried to make light of the meal by telling the story of the waiter in the Chinese restaurant who had remarked: 'In India, sir, all fish is polluted,' shortly before my protozoic invasion.

My guest was a recent arrival and it was his first time overseas. He worked for an American petroleum company about to launch a range of lubricants in India.

'It tastes more like . . . wet wood,' he decided after the second, hesitant mouthful.

If the way to a potential client's heart was through his stomach, thanks to my cook's dubious concoction I had reached his feet. 'Actually, it tastes like it's been fried in diesel,' I said with a contrived laugh. 'Poisson a la Derv.'

'Don't laugh,' he responded. 'This morning I met with some dealers from Pakistan. We've had our products there for several years. Recently we improved the formula of our most popular lubricant. One of the dealers came up to me and said he's had numerous complaints because our diesel no longer tastes as good as it used to. Tastes?!! What are these guys doing with it? Wait till I tell Dallas.'

That I did not get his business I can blame only partly on the fish, or whatever it was. Nonetheless, I subsequently confronted the cook over his fishy fuck up.

'What kind of fish was it?' I asked.

'Fried fish, sir,' he replied.

'I mean what breed, what species, what . . .?' I was lost for words.

'Oh, I see, sir. It was bekti.'

'Bekti?'

'Yes, sir.'

'Well, it was inedible.'

'Thank you, sir. Wilbur not eat it either.'

Wilbur was a dog I could control, sometimes, but when a platoon of stray dogs moved into my neighbourhood I had no control. It was the season, according to George. By which I assumed he meant the mating season rather than the debutante's. One particular dog set up home close to my bedroom window and howled incessantly through the night. It caused a close to final firework to ignite in the dark recesses of my mind.

It happened again the second night and I dreamed, eyes wide open, of airports.

The following day I visited a chemist's and bought some sleeping tablets. Not for me. For the dog. I powdered them into some cardamom cream flavoured biscuits and instructed the chowkidar that when the dog started barking he should give him a biscuit.

It worked to a point.

As I climbed into bed the dog started barking. It barked, howled for several minutes then fell silent. Good, I thought, as I rushed to cram three nights sleep into one. Early in the morning I was woken by the sound of honking outside. It was George trying to get in. The chowkidar, peckish for a midnight snack, had chomped his way into an impenetrable sleep.

Margarine, Chips and Chewing Gum

The cardamon cream flavoured biscuits had been supplied by a new client, one of our first major wins. Actually, we had won several other pieces of business prior to this but they turned out to be conceptual rather than real accounts. One such phantom who haunted us for weeks was a video cassette company. The owner having picked us—but not because our agency possessed the right number of letters—asked us to come up with a brand name, something every agency hates. Trying to name a parent's offspring is no job for an outsider. The parent always knows best, especially if he or she is paying for it. We came up with a few names, then several, then hundreds. Finally, I sent him a present. I added a note: 'Please find over 80,000 names enclosed.' The present was a dictionary.

And then there was the margarine manufacturer . . .

Soft margarine was a relatively new concept and it was meeting a strong resistance from consumers who traditionally preferred butter. One company had introduced the product in Calcutta but with the lack of refrigeration it quickly turned into an oily goo. Now a company based in the Punjab had cracked the problem by adding a preservative and they invited us up to discuss their advertising. Because George was sick, for once genuinely, I travelled up with the general manager. The account director who had christened me Kneeel and launched me into my first adventure in India accompanied us.

It was a long drive and it was made even longer by the continual bickering of my two companions. As far as the general manager was concerned the account director didn't understand the first principles of advertising. As far as the account director was concerned he had difficulty understanding anything his superior said. It was like travelling with Laurel and Hardy.

We stopped for lunch at a service station in the northern reaches of Haryana. There was a shop in the foyer selling tourist trinkets and magazines. In the middle of the display cabinet was an air pistol which the general manager purchased on the grounds that 'there could be bandits ahead.' The prospect seemed to amuse him but it did little for my comfort zone.

'I thought during daylight hours it was safe?' I anxiously asked.

'You never know,' he replied with a chuckle.

'Very unlikely,' the account director chipped in. 'Anyway, being a foreigner you'll be kidnapped rather than killed,' he unnecessarily added.

We reached the margarine factory in the afternoon and were greeted by an old school friend of the account director. From his enthusiastic comments it seemed the business was ours, unless we were shot by bandits. All we had to do was present to his director.

'Present what?' I enquired.

'Your good selves.'

I ended up showing them some examples of our recent work, including the Himachal Pradesh campaign. They appeared to like what they saw and after a few questions gave us an assignment to come up with a new campaign.

'Let's go and celebrate,' the general manager suggested as we drove away.

In the nearest town we eventually found a liquor store, for once not branded 'English'. I asked for a bottle of gin and a crate of tonic.

'Tonics? What are these tonics?' asked the proprietor.

'The most palatable way of avoiding malaria,' I jested. He looked more confused. 'Tonic water. Fizzy,' I tried to explain.

'Tonic water? Fizzy?'

My general manager stepped in, explained something in Hindi and I was given six bottles of Limca.

We were booked into the Eagle Motel and Beer Bar which according to the account director was 'Punjab's finest.' To me, it looked like the archetype for the Bates Motel in the film *Psycho*. As I was reluctantly taken away to be shown my room the account director yelled: 'You're lucky, Kneeel. Your room has air-conditioning.'

It also had walls which looked like they had been covered with rye crispbread.

'Please don't put air-conditioner and heater on at same time,' my host cautioned.

This seemed like sensible advice and probably from the same philosophical school as 'don't drive with one foot on the brake and the other on the accelerator.' Only after he'd left did I realize that the heater in question was for the water. He was obviously worried about an overload.

I was not alone within my crispbread box. Squadrons of mosquitoes had already made it their home despite the window screens. I was to be their sacrifice and I had no tonics to protect myself. I repaired to the general manager's room; almost identical to mine except the management had used a kind of crimson porridge to decorate his walls. It was also mosquito-free. I sank several gin and Limcas. Probably a record in itself. On an empty stomach I started to experience a number of minor hallucinations. One of them was a Big Mac.

'Let's eat,' I pleaded.

The account director found the room service menu and passed it to me. Either I was drunker than I thought or the person who wrote it was drunker than he thought. It was supposed to be in English but most of the meals had been taken from an eye chart.

'What's an umlof?' I asked.

'Probably an omelette,' I was told.

The only meal I could find which was vaguely recognizable was an Eagleburger. So that's where the U.S. ex-Secretary of State had ended up.

'Tandoori chicken,' decided the general manager, though I couldn't see it on the menu.

While we were waiting for our order the account director's old school friend called round. A lot of toasting went on until I passed into another plane of consciousness. When I returned the client had left and the general manager was wildly waving the air pistol around. He fired a shot. The pellet hit a naked light bulb. The bulb remained illuminated. This was either one hell of an endorsement for the light bulb company or a dismal failure for the gun.

*

I ended up producing two campaigns for the margarine manufacturer. The first promoted the health angle. The client said it was too serious and lacked fun. So I wrote a line. ANYTHING BUTTER CAN DO WE CAN DO BETTER, and jam-packed it with fun. They liked that. They liked it so much they showed it to another agency.

Understandably, on meeting with my new, improved and genuine biscuit client I was alarmed when he suggested that in order to get to know his business better the general manager and I should visit his factory . . . in Punjab.

'There's a hotel nearby where you can stay, The Eagle Motel,' he innocently added.

In the trade such factory visits are known as 'orientation trips', or, if it involves going somewhere nice, 'a junket'. Nearly all of mine had belonged to the former. I dreamed of finding out how wine was produced in Australia or how rum was distilled on some romantic, Caribbean island, but instead I ended up inspecting such picturesque spots as an oil refinery in Liverpool or a bottling plant in a humid Hong Kong

One of my worst visits was to a frozen chip (as in fish and chips) production line in Scarborough, Yorkshire. There's something they use in the process which permeates every pore in the body. Weeks after my visit I still smelled as though I should be soaked in vinegar and wrapped in newspaper.

In those days, in England, account directors were wining and dining machines and the one who accompanied me to Scarborough had taken American Express for his middle names. We almost bought the train going up and a pre-ordered limousine took us to the factory where we were shown how potatoes become starch sticks. At the end of our tour we joined the managing director in his office. Canadian, but only one generation away from Scotland, he was canny and blunt. When my colleague left the room to answer a phone call he said to me: 'I know you guys are on a gravy train. Thing is, I can't get on it and I can't seem to stop it. All I know is that I'm paying for it.'

The account director returned looking oh-so-joyful and dreaming about his Remy Martins on the trip back home. 'Listen, pal,' the client turned on him. 'When you get back to London I want you to personally go through every invoice for the last seven years.

Should be thousands of them. And I want you to break down every ambivalent cost into its actual components. When you say "transferring to sixty video tapes, five hundred pounds" I want to know how much the studio costs, what the tapes cost you wholesale and the exact time spent doing the transfer. Clear?'

The account director nodded back like a broken robot.

'And "Entertainment",' the client continued, 'You're an advertising agency, not a night club. I want every grain of salt accounted for.'

About a month later the account director moved to another agency.

*

The biscuit client asked us for another meeting. He arrived late.

'Sorry to keep you waiting,' he apologized, 'but during the night someone stole the wheels off my Mercedes.' He appeared remarkably resigned to the theft. Even more remarkably, he was just as sanguine over the next piece of news he gave us. 'There's also been a flood in my Punjab factory.'

'A bad flood?' I asked as sympathetically as I could.

'Whole place is a metre under water. A lot of soggy biscuits.' He lit a cigarette. 'We could lose production for several weeks, if not months.'

I felt sorry for him. I felt sorry for myself. Was there a jinx haunting me in India? The crunchy cookie account had just become the soggy biscuit account.

'Will the insurance cover it?' my general manager asked.

'I don't have any insurance. It's never flooded in Punjab before,' he replied with a hollow laugh. 'Fortunately, we have another plant in Nagpur.'

'Where's Nagpur?' I asked not knowing I would soon be going there.

'Right slap dab in the middle of India,' said the general manager.

'Another thing,' the client went on, 'I know we discussed you handling my biscuit business but I've decided to give you my sweet account instead.'

'But we're gung ho on biscuits,' I protested, even soggy ones.

The confectionery side was a small, almost inconsequential part of his business and billing nothing like biscuits. Crumbs, in fact.

'You said you'd worked on sweets before, Mr Kelly. I value your experience.'

Since he was the first person to get my name right I demurred from any further comment. Not so my general manager.

'You need to put your money behind your biscuit brands. That's what you're famous for. Let the sweets hitch a ride,' he tried to reason.

'So you don't want my sweets?'

'We'd rather have your biscuits,' the general manager persisted.

'You can't have my biscuits,' said the client. They were beginning to sound like two school boys bickering in the playground.

'Why don't we handle both?' the general manager suggested hopefully.

'Because I have decided to employ two agencies. One for the biscuits. The other for sweets.'

The general manager played his last card. 'Well, give the other agency the sweets.'

The client let out a long sigh and turned to me. 'Would you like to visit our Nagpur factory?'

I'd had better offers but protocol dictated a nod of my head.

Next morning I asked Vikki to book me a round trip to Nagpur by plane, ideally by the same plane to minimize my stay there. Later he informed me I could only fly back.

'I don't understand. If I can fly back surely I can fly there?'

'Planes only go one way.'

This seemed improbable. Had Nagpur stockpilled every jet in the country? Subsequently it transpired I could have flown both ways but not on the day I wanted. So instead I reluctantly accepted a train ticket. Vikki assured me I would have a first-class, air-conditioned sleeper and that the journey would take under seven hours. It proved to be yet another, uncontrolled experiment with the truth.

Indian Railways carries over eleven million people every day and it felt like most of them had congregated at the New Delhi station that afternoon.

'Don't forget to lock your case up, sir,' George warned as he dropped me off.

'It is locked.'

'No, sir. You need to padlock it to your bunk or someone will steal it.'

'I don't have a padlock.'

'You'll be able to buy one on the platform,' he assured me.

I had arranged to meet two of my colleagues at the station—the general manager and Gautam, one of my senior copywriters—but amid the thousands there was no sign of them. I eventually tracked down an official and showed him my ticket.

'Go to platform eight and look for your name on the reservation chart,' he said.

Platfrom eight was even more densely populated than the rest of the station. Hundreds of families had set up camp, perhaps permanently, and large bundles of sackcloth made progress in any direction difficult. I saw a sign in English and pushed my way over to read it: DO NOT EAT/DRINK ANY THINS OFFERED BY ANY CO-TRAVELLER/STRANGER WHILE TRAVELLING IN THE TRAIN.

This was not what I wanted to read.

What I wanted to read was: WELCOME TO NEW DELHI RAILWAY STATION, MR KELLY, YOUR FIRST CLASS, AIR-CONDITIONED BUNK AWAITS.

When I tracked down the reservations chart there was no sign of MR KELLY or even a KEDDY, CURLY, CHILLI, KAY LEE or any of the other pseudonyms I'd acquired during my stay in India. I looked at my watch. The train should have left five minutes ago.

'Is this the train to Nagpur?' I urgently asked another official.

'It is, sir.'

'Well, I have a first class ticket and can't find the carriage.'

He looked at my ticket, then looked at the train. 'No first class on this train. Must be a mistake,' he decided and wandered off before I could ask him how the mistake might be rectified. Whistles were being blown, doors were being slammed, people were starting to wave good-bye. Then I saw Gautam jumping up and down some ten metres or so away.

'We thought you were going to miss the train,' he said relieved to see me. Gautam had a beard so large it could have made a home for a flock of birds. He had been educated in England and spoke with an impeccable English accent. He guided me to our compartment which, when the six seats were converted, contained four bunks. The general manager was already squeezed into the corner dressed in a lime green track suit and fast asleep. Three other passengers sat opposite him.

'I think there are too many people. This compartment is only supposed to sleep four, isn't it?' I discreetly said to Gautam.

'Trains in India always begin crowded. No big deal,' he loudly replied. Perhaps like cereal packets the contents would settle once the train began moving.

'I guess, looking on the bright side, it's only a seven hour journey,' I said as I squeezed in next to Gautam.

'Seven hours? Ho. Ho. Who told you that?' he chuckled.

'Vikki.'

'Seventeen hours more like. Could be longer.'

'Seventeen hours!' I was aghast. 'It's only, what, eight hundred kilometres to Nagpur?'

'You've never been on an Indian train before. They're not noted for their speed. They can stop anywhere. For hours, sometimes.'

Ours suddenly started with a jolt a good half hour after the schedule had promised. Out of the dust-stained window I watched as dusk descended on Delhi until it became the dark countryside.

'Excuse me, sir. Which country do you belong to?' one of the three men sitting opposite politely enquired.

'England, originally. But I live in Delhi.'

'England? So you must like cricket.'

I didn't like cricket, least of all how my country had been playing it over the past couple of years, which included losing a test series to India. 'No, not really,' I replied.

With cricket out of the way that only left politics or sleep. Unless the three strangers intended to share the same bunk sleep was also out of the question.

'I'm going for a walk,' Gautam broke the silence.

'I'll come with you,' I willingly volunteered.

He pulled back the tattered sack curtain and we stepped out into the packed corridor. The train was basically a large, crowded and noisy village on the move. We pushed and shoved our way to the end of the carriage. PLEASE HELP THE TRAIN TO REACH ITS

DESTINATION requested an enamel sign by the toilet.

'Hang on,' said Gautam as he disappeared inside. He returned ten minutes later waving a lighted joint. 'This should do the trick,' he promised.

It was strong, could have been used as an anaesthetic. After a few puffs I had no idea whether I was travelling to Nagpur, Neasden or Neptune. Nor did I really care. I vaguely returned to our compartment to find that the three strangers had become one. We all now had a bunk. Unsteadily I climbed into mine. I was ready to sleep for hours, maybe days, but Gautam wanted to talk politics.

'See, what this country needs is a benevolent dictatorship,' he began controversially. 'I'm not alone in that belief,' he insisted. 'Last week there was a poll in the newspaper. Sixty per cent, almost two-thirds, share my view.'

'The trouble is,' I heard myself distantly answering, 'that most dictators aren't benevolent.'

'We need a strong leader, benevolent or otherwise. Someone who can kick our arse. Under Indira Gandhi's Emergency Rule at least things worked better. Even the trains ran on time.'

This has always struck me as a strange yardstick for judging a society's well being: whether the trains ran on time or not. In Germany the trains ran on time even while six million Jews were being exterminated. 'Rather than a dictator surely you need politicians who can be held accountable?' I suggested, or think I did.

Gautam lit a cigarette ignoring the NO SMOKING sign. Our general manager and the sole stranger remained motionless on their bunks. 'See, politicians in India are basically corrupt mobsters,' he said. 'They agitate crowds and turn them into mobs. Look what happened at Ayodhya and the destruction of the Babri Masjid mosque? The politicians were behind it, stirring up the hatred. "Do not shed blood, shed hatred", Indira Gandhi said.'

For a man who had inhaled enough dope to stun a hippo I was impressed by his articulation. 'You obviously admire Indira Gandhi,' I said.

'No, I don't admire her. The Gandhis ran this country like a family business. All I'm saying is that she was a necessary evil.' He stubbed his cigarette out on the floor. 'I tell you, unless we get a strong leader this country will become a huge Bosnia.'

'I think you're exaggerating,' I hoped.

'Not when my daughter asks me—she's only eight, mind—whether it's true that Muslims eat Hindu children.'

We sat in silence for a while listening to the clickety-clack of the train. Then our general manager stirred, sat up in his bunk and asked me all bright-eyed and bushy-tailed: 'So, what's gone wrong with your cricket team?'

*

Nagpur is famous for its oranges and for being located at the geographic centre of India, otherwise it looks like any other large, Indian city. The train spent an hour patiently waiting outside its environs as though a message had been sent to the driver that the city was not yet ready to receive visitors. Whatever the reason for the further delay, as we shunted into the station and stopped opposite the LADIES URINAL, I had been on board for almost nineteen hours.

Having declined 'any thins' offered by strangers, even though one, I was assured by a freshly charged-up Gautam, bore tin trays of mush from the train's kitchen, I was starving. But there was no sign of any food source, just a large I SPEAK YOUR WEIGHT machine with OUT OF ORDER plastered across its face.

We were welcomed by the brand manager (confectionery division); a cheerful, almost joyful Punjabi who had laughed at whatever I said during our first meeting in Delhi. Now he asked whether I had 'come with big ideas'. A hooker with an inquisitive, philosophical bent could have asked me the same question.

'I've come with a big hunger,' I responded. 'Can we get breakfast anywhere round here?'

He started giggling. 'You are what you eat,' he said evading my question.

'In that case I'm nothing,' I joked, provoking more giggles.

'At the factory you can eat as many biscuits and sweets as you wish,' he tried to tempt me. It was a small boy's dream come true. But I was not a small boy.

A biscuit factory is a biscuit factory even when it also produces sweets. The one outside Nagpur was little different from those I had visited in other parts of the world: a collection of interlinking cream buildings fronted by well-manicured green lawns. What set this one aside from the rest, however, was that at one end stood a small chapel, temple and mosque to cater for the different denominations of the work force: a reassuring symbol of religious harmony in a country that currently needed some reassurance.

'This is the most modern factory in India,' the brand manager enthusiastically told us. 'Here using the latest Italian machinery we produce biscuits, sweets and bread all to the highest standards of hygiène.'

Bread? My stomach growled in anticipation.

We were given white coats and chef's hats and introduced to the product manager who facially rather resembled a biscuit with his round face and two currants for eyes. While my stomach continued to grumble he took us through an endless supply of charts revealing his factory's output, diversification and growth. Finally, he offered us tea and biscuits. I wantonly gorged on the latter.

The first sweets we were shown being made were called Milk Drops, basically boiled sweets. They began life as a huge, glutinous blob then, after a process of extrusion, chopping and wrapping, they became more recognizable but nowhere along the line did milk make an appearance.

'Mango is our most popular flavour,' explained the product manager while sucking one. 'Followed by cardamom.' He handed out a handful for us to sample. I took several to add to my carbohydrate diet and dreamed of a meal that possessed more than one colour.

It took about an hour to complete the tour, the climax of which was a vast vat of latex destined to become chewing gum. I was given more samples. Then, frantically chewing, we were taken to the airport in one of the company's chicken soup, or caramel creme, Ambassadors.

'Maybe there'll be a restaurant at the airport?' I hopefully prayed aloud.

'Wouldn't risk it,' said Gautam. 'Wait until you get on the plane.'

But there was no plane. Just hundreds of waiting passengers.

'The plane's been cancelled,' the general manager informed us.

'Not postponed?' I begged.

He shook his head.

I groaned from hunger and despair. 'So what do we do?'

He glanced at his watch. 'We're in luck,' he said. 'If we really hurry we can catch the train back.'

My Tryst With Destiny

What is now called the Ferris wheel, I had read somewhere, originally came from India. It seemed an appropriate symbol for the relationship I had with my company, and at times with the country; going round in circles, frequently stranded in mid-air and occasionally having fun.

Jerry Della Femina, a legendary New York adman, once said 'Advertising is the most fun you can have with your clothes on.' Mind you, he said it over twenty years ago when advertising was enjoying its halcyon days. Then Creatives wore kaftans, had waist length hair, smoked dope for breakfast and had even more fun when they stripped and explored a secretary's anatomy under the board room table. It was during those heady days that I joined as a junior copy writer. Thereafter the fun began to slowly diminish. By the time I reached India it had almost disappeared.

But I hoped that in shooting my first Indian commercial I could rejuvenate it. Making a commercial was normally fun, especially if it involved travelling to some exotic South Sea isle with a bevy of beautiful blondes. My mistake, almost fatal as it turned out, was to set this commercial—for a new brewery—in 'the shimmering desert'. Had we shot it in the winter, when originally planned, it would probably have been all right. Instead, the client waited until one of the hottest months of the year before giving us the go ahead.

That's the problem with advertising: clients.

I had one in Hong Kong, an Argentine running a cognac company, who made my life hell and, ironically, over a blonde. I had written for him what I thought was a guaranteed fun spot for me. 'Open on stunning blonde crossing bridge in Paris,' was how it began. It had taken a lengthy, viticulous lunch to come up with this artistic gem and required another, even longer lunch once the client had approved it. Sadly, thereafter, it was downhill all the way. I arrived in Paris about the same time as a group of North African terrorists who proceeded to destroy while I was trying to create. Whatever location I found I could not get the necessary permit to film. The whole of Paris, it seemed, was off limits. To complicate matters still further there were no blondes. The majority had migrated to Tokyo to strut the catwalks. The remainder had been bagged by a team who had arrived earlier and who were producing a shampoo commercial. I was forced to go with a six-foot two, peroxide Amazon who looked transvestic and made the leading man, a boyish Spaniard, appear like her teenage son. Desperate, I eventually traced the client to a hotel in Monte Carlo.

'Can I speak to your daddy?' I asked the small voice who answered the phone.

'My father?' She sounded surprised. 'He's dead.'

'I'm sorry. I had no idea.' I was momentarily lost for words. With a dead client the shoot had also died. 'Er . . . forgive me for asking . . . when did he die?'

'About five years ago.' We were obviously not talking about the same man. I mentioned the client's name. 'Oh,' she replied instantly cheering up. 'You mean my husband. I'll get him for you.'

'This better be important,' he irritably announced on coming to the phone. 'I'm on my honeymoon.'

'Sorry to disturb you, and congratulations,' I mumbled. When I had last seen him in Hong Kong a month before, he had been married to someone else. 'I'm having a problem with the casting,' I told him. 'Blondes are out of stock. Now if we were to go with a brunette—'

'Absolutely not,' he snapped back. 'Asians want to screw blondes. Find a blonde.' And he put the phone down.

So I had no choice but to go with the tower of questionable femininity and changed the leading man for a taller, more mature Pole who I later discovered was incapable of swirling a brandy glass—the leitmotiv of the commercial. When the rest of the team arrived from Hong Kong, including a sullen Chinese director, all I could show them were the odd couple and a couple of less than satisfactory suburban locations.

'Shoot whole fucking thing in studio,' was the director's immediate reaction.

The rest of us reasoned we were in Paris, at considerable

expense, to shoot the real thing, not a cardboard cut-out. In response the director vanished for two days with a French sailor on shore leave.

Critical to the shoot was a spiral staircase. It was supposed to juxtapose with the swirl of brandy in the glass. After much searching we found a suitable location. Unable to contact the owner of the building we ended up bribing the concierge; a nervous, willowy man who thought he was still working for the Resistance. With the director back on duty we climbed to the top and began setting up the shot. There were lights and people everywhere which alarmed the concierge who had assumed we would be trespassing for minutes not hours. But when the director looked through the camera he was not happy. 'Move fucking carpet,' he fanatically ordered.

The concierge, now beyond alarm, fled from the building and it fell upon Jean Paul—a crusty member of the crew with a Gitane permanently smoking in his mouth—to remove the infinite number of runners. By the time he had finished a mountain of carpet had been piled up in the marbled foyer causing considerable consternation from the arriving tenants. Finally satisfied the director filmed our leading 'lady' swirling down the stairs.

I didn't see Jean Paul for several days. When I did he looked as though he had been tortured; which, to a point, he had. He explained how after we had left he had spent the night endeavouring to replace the yards of carpet. He was not assisted by the lights being on a time switch. Every time he tried to fit the runner he was plunged into darkness. But that was not all. None of us had noticed, including Jean Paul, that the stairs imperceptibly gained in width as they descended. By dawn he had fitted the runners but not in the right order. With dawn, also, came the return of the building's owner who irately insisted that unless Jean Paul wanted to pay for the cost of recarpeting the staircase he would have to work out the correct permutation.

It took him two days and, worse, three repeatedly interrupted nights to solve the cunning carpet puzzle. Besides missing most of the shoot, and all of his sleep, he acquired a morbid fear of all things helical, including the common corkscrew. This seemed particularly unfair given he was an inveterate wine drinker.

*

Wisely, I hadn't included a spiral staircase in my desert commercial which was required to launch not one beer but three, one as powerful as Thunderbolt. The owners of the brewery, identical twins who I never managed to differentiate, had no experience in this field and had made their money in the rag trade. Now they wanted to become beer barons even though their especially imported Danish hops had been indefinitely impounded (postponed) in a Madras godown.

'Mr Kelly has successfully launched beers in England, Scotland, Sweden and China,' my Indian partner had proclaimed at out first meeting.

'Yes, but he's in India now,' one of the brothers remarked, obviously unimpressed by my track record. 'It's a completely different market.'

Just so. And to celebrate its dissimilarity I penned my arid ode.

'The focal point of the commercial is to have this futuristic stainless steel fridge rising out of the desert,' I revealed at our second meeting.

'There's no electricity in the desert. How is the fridge supposed to stay cold?' one of them asked.

'We'll use dry ice to simulate the cold,' I replied. 'It's an old trick.'

'It's an old idea,' the other brother chipped in. 'I've seen the desert used before. Many times.'

Not again! Was I destined to spend an eternity in a plagiarist's hell? 'Okay,' I said with an exaggerated wink. 'There's this red Indian and he walks into a bar and says "How!" To which the barman offers him one of your beers and says "Now!" Then the red Indian, suitably amazed, replies "Wow!"'

The brothers blinked back at me in astonishment.

'Just a joke,' I lamely added, but neither laughed.

'Use a beach,' one of them eventually suggested. 'Beach and sea. Then you won't need a fridge. The sea will keep the beer cold.'

'Perhaps you should hear the entire idea first,' I said. They nodded with little enthusiasm. 'There are three heroes and a temptress. That's the cast. Each hero represents a different beer. There's a sophisticated, senior executive-type in a helicopter for the premium brand. Then we have a more casual guy, a sort of yuppie, in a sports car or four-wheel drive. Imported. He represents the medium brand. Finally, we have a muscular guy on a black horse for the rocket fuel.'

'Rocket fuel?'

'Figure of speech. I mean your strongest beer.'

'Helicopters are expensive?' the other brother enquired.

'I don't know. Once you approve the concept we'll get a quote. Anyway, the siren, the temptress, wills them towards the point in the desert where the futuristic fridge will rise out of the sand. We watch their progress. It's very, very hot. They're all sweating. They come together, the temptress disappears and is replaced by the fridge. It automatically opens to reveal the three different beers. Each hero grabs one. The film ends with the slogan: THE NEW BROTHERHOOD OF BEERS.'

There was a long pause.

'No shot of our brewery? It's state of the art,' one duly asked.

'I'm sure it is,' I agreed. 'But you don't show the tree, you show the fruit.' I could have picked a neater, less obtuse analogy.

'I see. And how about a magic moment?' his twin asked.

'A magic moment? The film's chock a block with them,' I replied.

'But are they magic enough?' he persisted.

'In my opinion, yes.' I tried one of my practised advertising smiles. It was supposed to instil confidence and exude charm, but sometimes it made me look like a recruiter for the Scientologists. 'Perhaps you would be kind enough to give me an example of what you consider to be a "magic moment"?'

'Well . . .' he considered. 'I don't know, you're the expert, but something like a small boy being presented with his first pet.'

'Might be hard to squeeze that image into this particular script,' I pointed out.

'Just an example,' he said.

I'm not sure where this notion of a 'magic moment' first came from. Clients refer to it as if it was some kind of Holy Grail, along with: 'Please make my logo bigger.' In Hong Kong, when I asked one client to give an example of a 'magic moment' he had replied: 'How about a man riding a donkey upside down?'

'Trust me,' I told the twins, 'this commercial is going to be truly magical.'

'Can we have time to think about it?' one of them requested.

'Of course.'

If this had been a movie the leaves of a calendar would have fallen off in clumps, for on this occasion time did more than take an overdose of valium. It picked up some chronic wasting disease and took to its bed. After waiting almost six months I decided they were either no longer a client or were no longer in business. But in India time waits for every man. As Rajasthan, our intended location, began notching up record temperatures one of the brothers called me out of the blue.

'Have you had any more ideas about how to sell our beers?' he ingeniously enquired.

'Well, no. To be frank, after all this time I wasn't sure we still had your business.'

'We've had a few production problems. Now we're ready to go. If that is still the best idea you have then please proceed with the shoot.'

As it turned out the helicopter did prove too expensive and it became a foreign jeep. The horse remained a horse and we added a 500cc motorbike. With sweat dripping on to the few location shots I had been sent I wished I had taken one of the brothers' advice and gone with the ocean. I also wished I had picked a different producer, as directors are called in India. My first, second and third choices had all given up waiting or crept over budget. The one I ended up giving the job to, an actor turned film-maker who worked out of his bedroom, initially appeared very enthusiastic about the project, promising me the earth and his total commitment. Then he returned to Bombay and ignored all further communications. A week before we were due to leave for Jaisalmer we still had no cast, no vehicles, no fridge, no cameraman, no final budget and no shooting schedule.

'Film producers in India follow a policy of ad hocism,' Gautam informed me. 'They take on too many jobs. Sometimes they have several going on at the same time.'

'Bad business . . . chaos . . . headache,' Gosh added in his inimitable way.

'But our producer appears to have taken a vow of silence,' I pointed out.

'Maybe he hasn't been paid his advance,' said Gautam.

'Money . . . agency . . . hah!' Gosh added.

My staff had begun studying me as some must have studied Jules Verne after his announcement that he intended to circumnavigate the globe. I wanted to take at least one of them hostage on this shoot. All, however, passionately insisted they had prior commitments. Except Gosh. Determined not to die alone I kidnapped a junior account executive. His name was Amit, a reluctant hero.

'It's your job to book the hotel and air tickets. We'll probably need an overnight stay in Jodhpur. Make sure the product gets there. The bottles must be perfect. Organize petty cash. Hire a car to get us around. Keep the client informed and start co-ordination with the production company who may, or may not, still be in the country,' I told him.

'I'll send a fax,' he said.

'It could take more than that.'

It was going to take a lot more than that.

Shortly before leaving for my tryst with destiny I had dinner with some friends. One of them knew the Maharajah of Jaisalmer reasonably well. She suggested I talk to him. He could possibly help in finding a horserider and even a foreign jeep. Later I called him. The voice that answered sounded very young. I almost asked if his daddy was in but knew better. 'Is that the Maharajah of Jaisalmer?' I enquired.

'Yes, yes it is.'

I explained who I was and what I was doing, or trying to do, and he recommended I contact a cousin of his in Jodhpur who was a professional polo player and very photogenic. However, he was unable to help with a foreign vehicle. I also asked him for the name of the best hotel in Jaisalmer which I rang next.

'About twenty people will be coming to shoot a commercial, an ad film, in three days time. We'll be there for a week. Do you have room?

'Oh, yes, sir. Most certainly. It would be a great pleasure to receive you.'

'Good. I'll get a man called Amit from my office to sort out the rates. The hotel's air-conditioned?'

'Very much so.'

'And it has a pool?'

'Correct.'

If nothing else, I reasoned, I would have a cool base to retire to every evening.

The day before I left the producer called me at home. He said, with a carefree chuckle, that he had failed to locate an imported car of any description. The best he could offer was his own 'modified' Gypsy.

'Modified in what way?' I tentatively asked.

'Spotlights, aerial, hub caps. That kind of thing.'

The average car dealer offered as much. 'To be honest, I'm disappointed. We've had months to find a vehicle.'

'Can't find what isn't there. I'll use wide angle lenses. Make it look dramatic.'

'And how about the fridge? You promised to send me a photo weeks ago. I have absolutely no idea what it looks like.'

'Don't worry,' he said with another chuckle. 'It looks great.'

Amit met me at the airport minutes before the plane's departure. He was carrying three boxes. I asked him if they contained bottles of beer.

'No,' he said, 'just the labels.'

'Labels? Why do we need so many labels?'

'I don't know.'

'So where's the product?'

'Coming direct from the brewery,' he replied, then quietly added: 'I hope.'

Amit was like a racing driver who had yet to acquire a car. He looked like an adman, even read *How to Succeed in Advertising* during the flight, but despite the research he had little idea about his role in the profession. For him, shooting a commercial was no different from shooting a duck. That he was to be my right hand man for a week in the flaming desert was a disquieting thought. But at least he had style. He had booked our accommodation that first night in Jodhpur in the Umaid Bhawan Palace: a vast and rambling, 350 room, art deco palace and one of the largest homes in the world. My bathroom could have garaged a small ship and given the size of the palace room service was more a case of a courier service.

I met the photogenic polo player later that evening in another, smaller palace. At first he declined my offer to make him a celluloid star but eventually vanity, and lucre, prevailed.

'Do you want me to bring my own horse?' he asked.

I told him what I had been told which was that we had one coming up from Bombay, a Bollywood star. It wasn't actually black as the script had requested but the producer had promised it would be on the day; apparently a simple transition involving boot polish.

The following morning we were due to leave for Jaisalmer at the crack of dawn. However, the crack became a chasm as we waited for our transport to appear. Denied the use of a fax Amit was forced to use the phone. He found out that the producer had arrived in the middle of the night and requisitioned our car. It was not until mid-day that a chicken soup 'Amby' trundled up the drive. Seven hours later, after a trip about as exciting as driving through Texas, we arrived at our hotel in Jaisalmer.

The hotel was a kind of White House resort. Like my former home it was still being built but parts that had already been constructed were going through an existential crisis. As we were checking-in there was an almighty flash.

'Good God! What was that?' I exclaimed.

The manager, who by the end of our stay would make Basil Fawlty seem positively congenial, dashed off to investigate. When he returned it was with the information that the generator had self-immolated. In this distant part of Rajasthan transmitted electricity was in short supply. With the generator down so was the air-conditioning. I began sweating. 'Where's the pool?' I asked.

'The swimming pool? It is not yet ready,' he replied.

'Not ready?' Had I caught it unprepared?

'It will be ready for enjoyment by winter.'

'What? I was told you had a pool.'

He mopped his own sweating brow. 'Yes, we indeed have a pool but a number of unavoidable delays have prevented us from completing it. I apologize for the inconvenience.'

No pool. No air-conditioning and, as we walked into the bar that evening, no gin. Taking our seats for dinner we further discovered there was next to no food. This wasn't a hotel. It was a notel.

'We have been awaiting deliveries from Jaipur,' the manager dejectedly provided another excuse. 'Please understand the management has recently changed hands and the necessary lines of credit are still being procured.'

Into this less than credible explanation walked the producer looking as relaxed as I felt agitated. He urged us to join him for dinner and half an hour later we were dining al fresco in the 'Skyroom' overlooking the old walled city. It's owner was a retired army major whom everyone called 'Papa'. He was also our local production manager. Indirectly I tried to ascertain if he had any film experience.

'If you can organize men for battle, you can organize anything,' he confidently told me.

'So you've seen active combat?'

'Yes, in Kashmir. It was my last post before retiring. In 1990. When the troubles started.'

I visited the Valley eight months later and experienced a battered paradise stuck in a time warp. I stayed on a houseboat where the magazines and guest register ended in 1989. I was the first guest that year, it was June, and the owner had been forced to sell his gold, wife's jewellery and finally his boat to stay in business; to stay afloat on a lake, the Dal, which was rapidly shrinking due to encroachment and had recently started turning red in summer because of the algae prospering on the pollution. Red water and, after Saddam had set the Kuwaiti oil wells alight, black snow. It was as if some higher force was administering punishment, displeased about what was happening in this Eden.

One evening I had dinner with the chairman of the Houseboat Association. He had named his boat THE NEW NEIL ARMSTRONG.

'Has Neil Armstrong even stayed here?' I asked.

'Not yet,' he replied. He showed me a framed letter from Armstrong's secretary which stated that her boss 'has no intention of visiting Kashmir in the near future.' But my visit there had completed another circle, another revolution of the Ferris wheel. From my friend in Calcutta hearing Neil Armstrong land on the moon to a man who had taken the astronaut's name for his home. The Indian standing next to my friend in 1969 had said it was not his moon. He believed it now belonged to the Americans. My host in Kashmir, twenty-five years later, reasoned that Kashmir did not belong to India. Given its unique beauty, and the threat it was under, it belonged to the world.

*

On the morning of my second day in Jaisalmer I was told by a grinning Amit that the film crew and cast had mysteriously disappeared. He said they had left Bombay on the previous afternoon's flight and that the plane had landed safely in Jodhpur. No one had seen them since. The producer, as ever, seemed unconcerned that he, Amit and I could be the sole survIviors of this desiccated debacle.

'Don't worry,' he said, his standard response. 'If they had been killed we would have heard by now. Only bad news travels fast in India.'

They arrived late in the afternoon looking like affluent refugees. During their drive through the night their bus had left the road and been bogged down in sand. One I talked to maintained it had been deliberate. A farmer with a tractor had conveniently appeared out of nowhere and after hours of negotiation had extracted a high price to pull them free.

'Wouldn't happen in Bombay,' he said.

'There's no desert in Bombay,' I pointed out.

'Well, you know what I mean. In the north people only care about money.'

The temptress had already worked her seductive magic on the two leading men during their long journey. So much so that they immediately elected to share the same hotel room into which they eagerly vanished. While they were practising, or inspecting their parts, the producer, cameraman and myself drove out to look for suitable locations. We had a problem. The recent rains, heavier than normal, had turned the desert into a garden.

'You'll have to change the script,' the producer told me as if it was simply a matter of changing a shirt.

'No way!' I put my foot down. Easier to change the producer. 'Aren't there some dunes around here? They should still be arid.'

'Sam.'

'Sam?' I looked around. None of us were called Sam. 'Who is Sam?'

'Sam is the name of the last town before the Pakistani border. Classic dunes there,' the producer explained.

'Good.'

'No, not good. Foreigners aren't allowed there.' He rubbed the designer stubble on his chin. 'I guess Papa could fix it.'

We returned to the hotel to find the horse had arrived and so had the fridge. The latter looked like the Yeti in a body bag. With great ceremony it was pulled from the truck and pushed into an upright position. I waited nervously for it to be unveiled, or released.

'The star of the show,' the producer announced.

The packaging was pulled away and I stared at what appeared to be a relic of man's first attempt to build a manned rocket using a dustbin and a conical tin hat. Cargo cultists might bow down before it but I was less than impressed. It was far from futuristic and the stainless steel was a dull aluminium scorched by an inexperienced welder.

'Hell's teeth! It looks ancient,' I said.

'That's the alternative. We make it timeless,' the producer willingly improvised.

'But it's so undramatic.'

'We'll shoot from down low. Wide angle. The close-ups I'll be doing in a studio in Bombay.'

The door in the fridge was supposed to slide effortlessly open electronically. Instead, what we had was a man inside who pulled it open shakily to reveal his grinning face. It fact, such was the fondness for this *objet d'art* that after the shoot had been completed no-one would claim it. For all I know it still sits in the dunes: a riddle for future archaeologists.

'How's it going to rise out of the sand?' I enquired. 'It's about as sleek as an elephant.'

'I've decided it won't rise out of the sand,' the producer suddenly decided. 'It will haze-on.'

'Haze-on?'

'Like a mirage. We'll fix all that in post production.' Then having instructed that the fridge be moved to the dunes he wandered off to meet the horse.

I returned to my room convinced I was about to slip off my ice cube in some remote corner of a foreign land. Picking up a locally produced guide book I realized I wouldn't be the first. 'I don't presume to be a scholar of English,' I read in the introduction, 'hence some mistake of expression might have crept in, which the wise readers will overlook as the proverbial swan rejects water and imbile the milk.'

That evening the twenty or so of us dined at the 'Skyroom'. Every shoot I had been on before was dry until the wrap party at the end. Not this one. Bacchus was amongst us and everyone, except me, drank and danced until two in the morning, even though we were due to start filming three hours later. The temptress, taking her part far too enthusiastically, tried to seduce everyone, except me. But what concerned me the most was the state of the cameraman who seemed determined to drink us all under the table. How would he be able to focus or hold the camera steady?

'Don't you think the cameraman's had enough?' I asked the producer who certainly had.

'He's fine. I've worked with him before. Always drinks a bottle of whisky before going to bed. Don't worry.'

I started worrying more than ever.

I was up at five the next or same morning. Before the sun and way before anyone else. At nine a few people started drifting into the restaurant, red-eyed and hungover, only to be told that eggs were off, bacon was off and even the chef had gone off to try and secure supplies. By now the manager had mastered the art of becoming invisible. His assistant, ever-smiling, had managed to learn a few basic words of English which, when strung together, encouraged his enraged guests to 'have a nice day.'

The producer was one of the last to appear. Sporting tinted glasses, his stubble no longer designed, he urgently ordered a pot of black coffee.

'Weren't we aiming for a dawn start?' I said as sarcastically as I could manage.

'Break them in slowly,' he mumbled lighting a cigarette.

'I think they're already broken. Have you seen the cast? They look like they've just got off a fourteen hour flight.'

'They'll be wearing sunglasses.'

'What, including the temptress?' It was her eyes, above all else, which were supposed to lure the three men to their beery end.

'We'll shoot her tomorrow,' he said. He poured himself a cup of coffee and took a sip. 'Yuck!' he winced. 'Tastes like hot oil.'

Eventually, lubricated back into life, the producer ordered his team to set off towards Sam.

'Exactly where are we filming?' his assistant asked.

'The place we saw yesterday.'

'We saw lots of places yesterday.'

'Just follow me.'

Cameraman and producer led the pack in the black Gypsy which had been minimally modified. Several times they stopped as if involved on a treasure hunt. Finally, they found the place or a place to begin filming. Since the photogenic polo player had yet to arrive we began by shooting the motorcyclist; sadly, with a camera and not a gun. All he had to do was ride the bike across the barren landscape. I'd asked him earlier if he could ride and he had assured me it was second nature, boastfully adding: 'I'm the James Dean of India.' Rebel Without a Cause in his case became Rebel Without a Clue. During the rehearsal he managed to snap a vital part of the gear box which involved flying up a mechanic from Bombay, costing us two valuable days in the process.

So we moved on to the Gypsy.

'I reckon this should be a wide shot,' I suggested to the producer. After setting up he invited me to look through the camera. 'It's not wide enough,' I said.

'In India it is,' he replied.

'What? A wide shot is a wide shot, anywhere in the world.'

'Trust me. This is wide enough.'

'I want it wider,' I insisted. I left and probably sounded like a spoilt brat about to throw a tantrum. To placate me he taciturnly agreed but I made the mistake of not checking. Later, on seeing the finished film, I discovered his concept of width always won over mine.

We 'completed' the first day's filming by travelling a hundred kilometres to a lonely level crossing. This was a surprise since as far as I was concerned it was a location we had still to agree upon. Even more of a surprise: he decided to film the temptress.

'I thought you said we were going to start filming her tomorrow?'

'She looks okay. Besides, you won't see much of her because the train will be passing in front,' he reasoned.

On one side of the gates would be the hero in the Gypsy. As the train flashed past we would get a glimpse of her. She would vanish with the train, leaving behind a clue: an illustration of the fridge which someone had yet to draw. The train was due to pass at 5:17. This seemed a ridiculously precise time for a country whose trains are notoriously unpredictable. By 5:05 we were almost ready when a coach appeared and disgorged its load, a large group of Swiss tourists all armed with video cameras. Desperately, we tried to make them keep their distance but as far as they were concerned this was an inclusive part of their exclusive tour—a personal encounter with a Bollywood starlet. Eagerly they pressed forward, cameras whirring. I saw the train coming and took my place behind the only camera that should have been there.

'Get out of ze vay!' a thick accent yelled behind me. 'I'm trying to film ze girl.'

'Hey, pal! We're the only people supposed to be filming her,' I angrily retorted as the train thundered past. Then, to my horror, I noticed through the gaps in the carriages that one of the tourists had crossed the track and was filming the temptress in close-up. He had undoubtedly been included in our film.

'Cut! Cut!' the producer yelled in a falsetto shriek.

'When's the next train?' I asked his assistant. I assumed it would be in an hour or so.

'Same time tomorrow,' he replied.

The next day began better. A few supplies had been smuggled into the hotel and all the cast were on duty and looking comparatively human. We even departed before the sun had bleached the day out.

'What are we going to shoot this morning?' I asked the producer, tired of his secret or non-existent schedule.

'Drinking shots.'

We returned to Sam—an acronym, I had decided, for SOD ALL MOVIEMAKERS—to find that in our absence mysterious nomads, or Swiss tourists, had visited our shrine of a fridge and left numerous tell-tale foot prints behind. Someone had the bright idea of trying to eradicate them with a wind machine. Clouds of sand flew everywhere; into our eyes and, worse, into the camera.

'Kill that damn machine!' yelled the producer becoming as blunt and as autocratic as his Chinese counterpart in Paris.

The second attempt to return the dunes to their pristine state proved no more successful. This involved a team using squares of cardboard scraping away the old prints only to leave a fresh set behind.

'We'll shoot the heroes from waist up,' the producer

compromised, thus making the dunes little more than an ocherous blur in the background. The way things were going we could have shot the whole production in a studio. At least the beer would have been cold. In the heat of the desert it was, understandably, hot and when poured, cloudy.

'The beer's no bloody good,' the producer told Amit.

'It's not my fault,' he protested. 'You said it was fine last night when you were drinking most of it.'

The motorcyclist thought it was fine, too. He downed several glasses of the strongest beer while practising his part. By lunchtime he was drunk and boisterous. Feeling that the photogenic polo player was a tad too photogenic and therefore a threat he began loudly insulting him. Insults turned into threats and as the two men squared off the Bollywood horse bolted.

'Shit!' uttered the producer close to panic. 'It's not insured.'

'Don't worry,' I grinned back.

*

Miracles do happen.

It was a miracle we ever completed the shoot and it was a miracle one or more of us didn't end up being buried next to the fridge. The motorbike was fixed, the horse found, fresh beer delivered and the level crossing sequence re-shot. That Amit resigned on returning to Delhi and the producer went way over budget were the only visible casualties of our war with the desert.

The filming was complete but the commercial still had to be edited. This the producer did privately in Bombay. By the time I was invited to inspect the result it was a *fait accompli*. It was also overlong.

'Your brief was to produce a forty-five second spot,' I reminded him. 'Why does it last a minute?'

'Too much material to cut into a forty-five,' was his laid-back response.

'So, if you went into a restaurant and ordered a snack and instead you were given a five-course feast, and when you complained the waiter said there was too much food in the kitchen to make a snack, would that be acceptable?'

'If I only had to pay for a snack, yes.'

I had not seen the client, the twin brothers, for months. Although I had invited them to the shoot they had wisely declined. Since our last meeting the script had changed fundamentally and increased by twenty-five per cent in length. The budget had stretched even more and I was still fighting with the producer over how the fridge should appear. He maintained he no longer had the money to create the 'haze-on' effect. I was therefore unsure of what kind of reception I would receive.

I presented in a room crammed with clothes waiting to be exported to the European winter. Just as I started playing the commercial there was a power cut. After a few minutes the generator kicked in but with less voltage the colours on the television looked pale and washed out. The video machine also operated at a slightly slower speed. Together we watched the world's first stretchy, bleachy television commercial.

There was a nerve-wracking silence after it had finished.

'Well, what do you think?' one brother asked the other.

'I think it's . . . ' he paused and my heart performed a frenetic drum solo. ' . . . much better than I expected.'

Hallelujah!

For once, it seemed, I had grabbed victory from the jaws of defeat rather than the other way round. The Ferris wheel was spinning and I was rising to the top.

One of the Crowd

Most mornings George and I would drive past an electronic billboard on Delhi's inner ring road which records India's growing population. The last digit changed in less than a second. Keeping a mental note of the ever increasing figure I worked out that a million Indians were born every fortnight. Put another way, the population of Delhi was being reproduced every five months. Put still another way, if the United States, three times the size of India, had the same population density it would be home for nearly three billion citizens.

'That's the problem with this country, sir. There are too many people. People, people everywhere. And there's not enough food to go around. That's the other problem,' was George's appraisal of the situation.

I regarded his size. 'You seem to get by.'

'Not really, sir. I'm empty inside.'

Certainly, the population in the jhuggi next to Kum Kum had started to grow in geometric proportions. Every day new arrivals appeared and created homes out of wood, tin and hope. I was now surrounded on three sides, frequently four when twenty or more played cricket outside my front gate, yelling and screaming as they dreamed of one day playing for their country. Some of the women took in washing which they would thump dry during the day and at least once a week the growing community would celebrate a forgotten festival into the early hours of the morning. I never felt lonely.

George, however, saw this rise in the local population as a hostile army gaining strength. 'You should have got rid of them in the beginning,' he said gloomily. 'Now they're everywhere, sir.' He pointed up at the illegal electricity cable. 'And they're still tapping your electricity.'

I had mentioned this point to the office manager several times but he had done nothing about it. Then again, I hadn't received an electricity bill since the one which had amused the ex-chowkidar so much. It seemed we were all getting free electricity—when we weren't getting power cuts.

'They mean no harm,' I tried to assure him.

He shook his head. 'They're dangerous people, sir,' he insisted.

'What evidence do you have of that?'

'Yesterday, the cook told me they had threatened to kill him.'

'Why, have they tried his food?' I joked.

'I'm being serious, sir. They don't like Christians.'

Along with George, the cook and his family were Christians. And their servant. So was I, to a point. I wasn't sure what Freddy the chowkidar believed in. Voodoo? The mali was surely a moon worshipper.

'He's very worried,' George continued. Which meant he was very worried.

'We'll be fine. Don't worry.' I had obviously picked up the producer's relaxed attitude after our time together in the desert. Besides, we had Wilbur to protect us. And an unlimited supply of stretchy, thumpy music. If the American government had successfully forced dictators into submission by playing very loud rock music outside their homes, I was sure a deafening onslaught of Megadeth's extended hits would keep any potential miscreants at bay.

'You just don't understand these people,' George concluded. Once again, as when we were trying to remove the recalcitrant chowkidar and he had made the same remark, I half expected him to peel off his face and reveal a mesh of wire and flashing transistors. The Driver from Planet Drog.

That Saturday afternoon a vociferous team started erecting a huge marquee outside the front gates using some of the iron spikes as pegs.

'They've said it will go on all night,' George, legs full of fresh stress, came rushing into the house to tell me.

'What will go on all night?'

'The wedding. Outside.' Failing to solicit a reaction he added: 'There'll be music. Very loud. And fireworks.'

I had already let off most of my cerebral ones. It was time I enjoyed someone elses.

'Terrible business,' George promised.

'If it gets too much, we'll leave.'

'The road will be blocked. We have to leave now.'

'Not that I intend to, but if we did where would we go?'

'You could visit my house, sir.' He put on one of his most pleading looks. 'It's my youngest son's birthday.'

The cook passed. I asked him what was for dinner.

'Fish, sir.'

*

George's home was on the outskirts of West Delhi. Driving there made me realize how large the capital had become. In population terms alone Delhi had grown from 800,000 in 1947 to currently around ten million. In common with Los Angeles it had spread like an oil slick. Unlike L.A. it lacked a geometrical structure; and, for that matter, an infrastructure. Buildings had been randomly thrown up and roads added later. Some of these roads, unable to find an exit, ended up at someone's front door and then continued on from the back of the house. Nor did the numbers follow any logical sequence. As I discovered while searching for a home of my own, houses had acquired their number according to the order in which the plots had been sold. Hence number 54 would be sandwiched between 19 and 92.

'How do you get home every day?' I foolishly asked George after we had been driving for nearly an hour. 'With great effort, sir,' he was only too keen to reveal. 'It involves several buses. Sometimes the buses don't connect and it can take well over two hours. If only I had a mobike—'

'Life is full of if onlys George,' I quickly interrupted.

We finally arrived by backing up a narrow, dirt cul-de-sac. Chez George was a small hut measuring about four metres by three. There was a dusty courtyard outside with a dead palm in an earthenware pot and lines of limp washing. A worn curtain packed with faded nursery rhyme animals concealed the outside toilet.

'Welcome, sir,' George said as his family appeared to greet me. 'This is Mrs George,' he introduced his wife. Bypassing his eldest son and two daughters he introduced his youngest son. 'And this is Augustine. Tell Uncle how old you are today.'

In response Augustine burst into tears. Maybe he didn't want a Caucasian relative.

'Now, now Augie,' Mrs George tried to pacify him. 'Birthdays are supposed to be fun.' Over his tears she added, 'He's five.'

'Come inside, sir,' George suggested. He placed the still sobbing Augustine on his shoulders and led the way.

After the outside glare the interior was as dark as a stomach. As my eyes grew accustomed to the gloom I saw that the walls were covered with religious icons, including a torn and garish poster of Christ on the cross. Boxes and a few pillows were the only evident furniture. A pot was steaming on the stove.

George asked one of his daughters to fetch a chair which she did, from somewhere, and it was placed in the middle of the room. 'Sit down, sir,' he said. I sat down and became literally the centre of attention. George dragged an old tin chest from out of the corner, opened its lid and began proudly showing me faded photographs of his time in the army, his brief boxing career and his stay in Iraq where he had worked as a foreman on a construction site.

'I should have stayed there, sir. The money was good, very good,' he mused staring at the photograph. 'I was not designed to be a driver.'

'George!' his wife admonished.

Feeling the tension I changed the subject by asking where they all slept. My question prompted an immediate demonstration. Coir mattresses appeared as if out of nowhere and were spread across the floor until they covered it, making one, large communal bed. Then they all stretched out like toy soldiers in a box.

'But he snores,' Augustine, no longer crying, said of his father.

'Yes, none of us get much sleep because daddy snores so loudly,' the rest of the children chorused.

George looked uncomfortable. 'I enjoy my sleep,' he said in defence.

'Boring. Boring. The old man is snoring,' one of his daughters began chanting.

'Enough!' George scolded her. 'Anyway, sir, would you like a drink?'

'Sure, why not? Thanks.' I waited to see what kind of potion he would produce given he had said he never drank himself. To my alarm it was a bottle of Thunderbolt. He poured half of it into a glass and handed it to me. After a couple of sips I was ready to drive an onion truck to Jaipur.

'Did you bring your passport?' George suddenly asked.

'It's in my briefcase, in the car. Why?' Were we all about to emigrate together?

'The children like looking at passports,' he explained. Then he added a heaped spoonful of pathos. 'It's probably the closest they'll ever get to travelling abroad.'

My briefcase was brought from the car and I handed my passport to Augustine. His brother, sisters and mother crowded around.

'. . . requests and requires . . . in the name of Her Majesty . . . to allow the bearer . . . to pass freely . . . without let . . .' the oldest son attempted to read out from the 'request' printed inside the front cover. Once, stuck in Tangier, having had my money and air ticket stolen by a kleptomaniac Arab, I presented this diplomatic ultimatum to a Moroccan policeman, taking him slowly through each word and emphasizing the part which states: 'to afford the bearer such assistance and protection as may be necessary'. In response he had laughed and torn free the page containing my photograph, rendering my passport useless and causing me days of bureaucratic hassles.

'Hong Kong . . . Australia . . . New Zealand . . . Japan . . . Thailand . . . USA . . . Malaysia . . . Egypt . . .' they eagerly shouted out my visas and stamps as Mrs George slowly turned the pages.

'Your passport's almost full, uncle. Then you won't be able to go anywhere,' George's oldest son announced.

Augustine started to cry again.

'Don't cry, it's your birthday,' I said to him. 'What would you like? I'll buy you a present.'

He immediately stopped crying. 'Fireworks!' he yelled.

'Is there a shop nearby?' I asked George.

'Yes, sir. Ten minutes drive from here.'

The four children plus two friends and an enormous doll all squeezed into the car along with George and myself. An instant crowd.

'Do we need any fizzy drinks?' George asked his wife.

'Yes, but don't go to Mr Khan's. His cold drinks aren't cold,' she called back.

We set off to the sound of George's favourite cassette: *The Best of Jim Reeves*, which had not only stretched but because the car's stereo player was so full of dust sounded like a musical fog horn. Despite its unintelligible rhythm, George sang happily along.

'People say I look like Jim Reeves, sir,' he self-consciously told me. I examined him and couldn't see the slightest resemblance.

'I don't think your tape sounds too much like Jim Reeves. It's stretched,' I said.

'You mean it's not supposed to sound like this?' He looked dismayed.

'Daddy, this music's horrible,' his oldest daughter squealed. 'Play some Apache Indian.'

'Michael Jackson,' another screamed.

'Uncle, how many fireworks are you buying me?' Augustine demanded to know.

'Uncle will buy as many as he thinks wise,' his father replied. Then he returned to his dissonant recital.

George had said the drive to the firework shop would take ten minutes. I should have known, being in India for as long as I had, that any time quoted for a journey was not to be taken too literally. And the longer we drove the more Augustine fidgeted. As his father tacked round a corner rather too fast he was violently sick.

'He always gets car sick,' his father cheerfully explained. 'That's why he'll never be a driver when he grows up.

'Oh, I don't know. I've met sailors who get sea sick,' I said not wishing to see his youngest son lose a possible career.

'I don't want to be a driver when I grow up,' Augustine announced on the verge of tears again.

'I don't blame you,' his brother chimed in. 'There's no money in it. You have to lie about your overtime like Papa does.'

*

Indian fireworks are basically live ammunition. A few rupees will buy a bomb, mortar shell, grenade, a string of explosives or even a miniature SCUD missile. Most fireworks are bought and detonated during Diwali, the colourful and noisy festival marking the return of Ram from voluntary exile, but at any time of the year distant bangs punctuate the night.

The arsenal we visited was run by an old man with a threadbare beard and an allergy to something—perhaps children—since he never stopped sneezing. He regarded our request for fireworks as if we were terrorists, but eventually pulled an old cardboard box from behind the counter which the children began impatiently raking through. I bent down and picked up one of the boxes. It contained, I read, MAGIC FOUNTAIN MIGHTY ATOM. On the side of the box was the warning: HOLD THE DUMMY END. LIGHT OTHER END AND LET HAND LEAVE BODY. Maybe 'Dummy' should have been put at the end of the first sentence.

'These make really big bangs,' Augustine said. He showed me what looked like a chocolate, round and foil wrapped. The fuse appeared dangerously short. I bought him two boxes. One of his sisters grabbed a handful of rockets. Then Augustine wanted more bombs. George picked up a large box of chocolates, or perhaps they were also bombs. We forgot the soft drinks.

Reaching home the children eagerly showed Mrs George their purchases. George was more furtive. 'What have you got,' George?' his wife asked as he tried to hide the present in his tin chest.

'Chocolates,' he mumbled so indistinctly that he made it sound like 'Clock legs'.

'Speak up,' she told him.

'Uncle bought him a big box of chocolates,' the eldest son revealed.

'That's very kind, sir.' She turned to her husband. 'You make sure you share them. You need to lose weight.'

'No, I don't, George protested. 'Eating keeps me fit.'

'In that case,' smiled Mrs George, 'you must be the fittest man in India.'

'Can we let off the fireworks now? Please? Please?' begged Augustine.

'It's not even dark yet,' said his father.

'I don't care.'

'Just one or two, then,' his mother relented.

One or two quickly became twenty or more as we unleashed a formidable barrage. Within the four walls of the small courtyard the explosions were ear-splitting, but at least for once the fireworks were going off outside of my head. With the first bang a few faces appeared over the wall. Soon there was a curious crowd of thirty or forty cheering every explosion.

George glared back at his neighbours. 'See, sir. Everywhere in India there are too many people. I'm going inside to make some tea.'

He had been gone about half an hour when Augustine came running out of the house. 'Uncle. Uncle,' he said between sobs.

'What's the matter, Augustine?' I asked.

'Papa's eaten all the chocolates.'

Juggling With Tigers

There aren't many tigers left in India. There aren't many jugglers, either. I was looking for one of each to appear in a couple of commercials I had written. The juggler was supposed to juggle five flaming clubs, then lose his concentration because a small boy in the front row was tempting him with a Milk Drop from the factory in Nagpur. I knew jugglers existed in India (I was less sure about tigers) because I had seen one performing at a circus outside Delhi's Red Fort. And everyone had nodded when I'd asked if we would be able to find one. 'No problem.'

I gave the task of locating a juggler to a production company in Bombay. The producer told me he lived in the same building as a circus owner. He was sure the owner had several jugglers on his books. Meanwhile, I conducted my own search in Delhi. There was a toy shop in Khan Market which by way of a sideline kept a portfolio of children's entertainers. I asked the owner if he had a juggler.

'Indeed, sir. I have a very good juggler from Rajasthan,' he told me.

'Great. How many objects can he juggle with?'

'Depends what the objects are.'

'Clubs.' I decided not to tell him yet that they would be flaming.

'Clubs? Like golf clubs?'

'No, no. Conventional clubs. They look like bowling pins.' I crudely drew one on a piece of paper.

'Swords is his speciality. Wouldn't you prefer swords?'

'How many swords can he juggle with?'

'Three.'

'Three? That's not very impressive,' I said.

'Maybe with practice, four,' was his best offer.

*

I needed the tiger to endorse a credit card. I also needed a game resort which would accept the card. While the search for the juggler was continuing I headed south to the jungle sanctuaries at Bandipur, Nagarhole and Mudamalai. I flew to Bangalore first and met a friend who had been studying game parks in India for eighteen years. Together we drove to Mysore and spent the first night at the Kabini Lodge in Karapur. The lodge was run by John Wakefield, a British octogenarian who had spent virtually all his life in India. That evening, over a bottle of whisky, we discussed the possibility of spotting a tiger.

'It's not a good time of the year,' admitted John. 'Too dry. But we may be lucky.'

My friend reminded him how a few years earlier three American zoo directors had been paddling across the lake by Kabini, bemoaning the lack of tigers, when one had leapt into the water and swum towards them.

'It's always when you least expect to find one that you do,' John said.

While I was trying to eat my dinner I was told about the tiger's eating habits. Apparently, the tiger rarely consumes its kill at the scene of the crime but drags it off to a more suitable location. This is understandable. Humans don't tuck into their chateaubriands in the shadow of the slaughterhouse. Once in the right setting the tiger will prepare its dinner with the skill and dedication of a master chef. Skin, hair or fur are first removed along with the entrails then an incision is made so that the organs are exposed. Liver, heart and kidneys are a tiger's favourite. Like a dedicated gourmet a tiger prefers to dine alone and in silence. Nor do they rush their food. A typical tiger feast will last at least an hour during which it will ingest up to forty kilograms of meat. However, if a tiger's appetite for food is voracious it's sexual appetite makes Casanova seem celibate. During the mating season tigers will copulate as frequently as fifty times a day.

Our trip the following morning in John's Gypsy was, sadly, tiger free. We saw prey a plenty along with an angry elephant demonstrating, but if there were any tigers around they showed no interest in appearing in a credit card commercial. When we returned unrewarded to the lodge there was a message from the Bombay producer.

'I think we've found a juggler,' he said after I had returned the call.

'In Bombay?'

'No, in Patna. I'm sending one of my people over there to interview him and take some pictures. When are you back in Delhi?

'When I've found a tiger.'

'A tiger?'

'That's why I'm here. It's for another project,' I explained.

'Use stock footage,' was his solution.

*

I have no idea how many jugglers there were in India at the end of the nineteenth century but it has been estimated there were over 40,000 tigers. By 1972 their numbers had shrunk to less than 2,000. British sahibs and Indian princes had in the name of sport hunted the species close to extinction. They rest in Sussex now, those pith-helmeted men of Kipling, or in hill station graveyards. They, too, are close to extinction but during their heyday they turned thousands of tigers into rugs and wall ornaments. The latest census puts the tiger population at around 3,750. But it may be considerably less, thanks to the poachers who illegally satisfy the huge demand in East and South East Asia where it is widely believed that eating tiger makes the libido roar.

For three days we roamed the sanctuaries looking for Sher Khan.

'I don't believe they exist,' I said half jokingly. 'It's a scam by the Tourist Board to get tourists to explore areas that would otherwise remain unexplored.' I had once said the same thing about the kangaroo, having spent a day driving round the Australian Outback in, of all things, an old Rolls Royce,with a Methodist farmer who was determined, for the sake of national pride, to prove it did exist.

We drove back to Bangalore without ever seeing a tiger, not even a cat.At the hotel there was a fax from the Bombay producer:

'Missed circus at Patna. My man now gone to Bhubaneswar.'

'It's the capital of Orissa,' my friend revealed. 'A city of five hundred temples.'

'And at least one juggler, I hope.'

Back in Delhi my confectionery client was becoming as concerned as I was over the lack of progress in finding a juggler. Nor was our concern alleviated when the owner of the Khan Market toy shop appeared at Kum Kum with his Rajasthani juggler in tow.

'He can now do four swords,' the owner proudly revealed.

'Okay, let's see.'

We walked on to the lawn and the juggler pulled the props out of his bag. He started with one, moved to two and uncertainly graduated to three. Sensing a possible suicide the children from the jhuggi next door climbed up to look over the garden wall.

'*Char*! *Char*!' yelled the toy shop owner, urging him to include the fourth sword.

The juggler's face took on a look of absolute constipation, and I don't mean concentration, as he desperately tried to create a gap for his fourth sword. At which point Wilbur came leaping over the flower bed to attack this curious apparition. For a moment it was as if the swords remained suspended in mid-air as the juggler ran for safety. Then they came clattering down with one narrowly missing Wilbur. The children cheered.

The dog was secured and the toy shop owner eventually persuaded the juggler to make a second attempt. As before he moved from one, to two, to three.

'He's getting very close to that cable,' I pointed out as the juggler started throwing his three swords ever higher. My warning went unheeded.Both Juggler and his boss were far more concerned with creating a foursome. There was a flash. The children screamed and disappeared. For months I had been asking the office manager to sever the illicit wire tap. Now an amateur juggler had done it for me.

'You're not looking in the right place,' my general manager casually informed me one morning. 'Madras, there's loads of jugglers there.'

I felt like asking him why he hadn't suggested that location in the first place but let the matter pass. He contacted our Madras office and the search, in effect, became nationwide. They reported back several days later saying they had found one called Anthony. They were going to set up a screen test and send us the results. I explained we were looking for someone who could juggle at least five objects and that they should be flaming.

'No problem,' I was assured.

Meanwhile, I had resolved the problem with the tiger by making it an elephant. I had also turned the commercial into a print advertisement. My client in Singapore, who had enjoyed such a meagre night's entertainment in Delhi, at first seemed less than happy with the compromise.

'I don't know. A tiger has so much more mystique. Elephants have been done to death.'

'No, it's tigers that have been done to death. There are hardly any left,' I corrected him. 'You'll love the elephant once you see it.'

The screen test arrived from Madras at about the same time as another fax from the Bombay producer. 'Bad news, I'm afraid,' I read. 'Juggler at Bhubaneswar no good. There is another circus currently at Chandigarh which has a juggler. Will investigate.' The screen test, however, offered a glimmer of hope. This man, at least, could juggle with four tennis balls. I called the Madras office.

'Can he juggle with five?' I asked.

'He says so.'

'But, for the film, he needs to juggle with flaming objects. Obviously, they cannot be balls.'

'Why not?'

'How's he going to catch them?'

'Perhaps he can wear asbestos gloves.'

'I don't think that will work. Try some clubs.'

'No juggling clubs in Madras, just drinking clubs.'

'I meant wooden clubs.'

'Oh, those kind of clubs. We'll try.'

'Of course,' I said wearily to the general manager who had overheard my conversation, 'we could always resort to animation.'

'Never give up. Rome wasn't built in a day.'

'The Romans didn't have a furious client breathing down their necks,' I said.

As it turned out Anthony didn't try clubs, nor did he wear asbestos gloves, but he did attempt to juggle with five flaming tennis balls.The inevitable consequences were filmed, which I watched with a combination of amazement and horror a couple of days later.

'Success at last,' the Bombay producer called to tell me. 'We've found an excellent juggler.'

'Good. Where is he?' I asked.

'In Madras.'

'Don't tell me his name is Anthony?'

A pause. 'Actually, yes it its. How did you know?'

The commercial was finally shot while I was away in the States using a juggler from Kerala who, in truth, could neither act nor juggle; though after hundreds of takes he eventually managed to keep three flaming sticks long enough in the air for the camera to film them. The key boy who was supposed to tempt the juggler with an irresistible Milk Drop had about as much charm as Freddy, my chowkidar, and the other kids all looked comatosed.

Not that any of this really mattered because the producer in Madras had decided to produce India's first, abstract commercial. It had a beginning, middle and end but not in that order. The accompanying jingle had suffered a similar fate and sounded like someone repeatedly throwing handfuls of coins down a flight of concrete stairs. I should not have jested. Using animation would have been a much better solution.

'I'm sure we can fix it,' I told the disappointed client at a meeting on my first day back. 'Just needs re-cutting, have a look at some of the shots that haven't been used, and record a new music track.' I felt like I was telling a new home-owner that his house would be fine once the walls were knocked down and the roof removed.

'If you say so.' He didn't sound at all convinced.

'But the spot has already run,' the general manager suddenly decided to inform us.

'What?!' the client exploded, 'Why?'

'Why?' echoed the general manager. 'Why . . . because we had nothing else to run in its place.'

'Well, please make sure it doesn't run again,' he instructed.

The general manager summoned the media manager who in a previous life, I'm sure, had cheerfully sat knitting while heads rolled off the guillotine. In her current embodiment when she executed a media plan the consequences could be almost as fatal.

'The client doesn't want the Milk Drop film to run anymore. At least not until it's been revised,' the general manager explained to her.

'I see,' was all she said.

'You understand?'

'I do.'

'So you'll cancel the rest of the plan?'

'Cancel or postpone?'

'Cancel.'

'Not postpone.'

'No.'

When I was a child there used to be a compere on television who made a living by trying to force contestants to say 'yes' or 'no' during a conversation with him. Once they said either they were knocked out of the competition. It seemed that game had reached my agency.

The plan was cancelled and so, not long after, was our association with the Nagpur sweet company. We had earned little from the relationship but I had learned a valuable lesson. Along with babies, jugglers should not be written into a commercial. Oh, and add spiral staircases, desert locations and tigers to the list.

*

Nevertheless, I was still determined to see a tiger in the flesh before I left India. One Saturday morning I asked George to take me to the Delhi Zoo.

'The zoo here is not as good as the one in Calcutta,' he replied.

'Maybe, but we're not in Calcutta,' I reminded him.

When we arrived at the zoo there was a solitary cow standing outside. Had it escaped? Was it trying to get in? Or was it simply curious? I said to George: 'How many cows do you reckon there are in India?'

He speculated intensely for a while, so much so that I expected him to deliver a reply precise to the last digit. Instead he said: 'I have no idea, sir. Too many. It's because in India you can't kill them. They're sacred.'

'That I know.' No hamburger hell awaited these emaciated icons.

I later discovered there are over three hundred million; the largest bovine population in the world and coincidentally, sadly, a similar number to the people still living below the poverty line. Another metaphor in the making. Because the ratio between cows and tigers shares a rough correlation with that of the powerless poor and the powerful rich.

Dehli's zoo is situated next to Humayun's tomb. Humayun was the second Mughal Emperor and father of Akbar. He died after falling down the stairs of his library, proving that a little knowledge can indeed be a dangerous thing. The zoo was opened in November 1959; receives more than a million visitors every year; contains over 1,600 mammals, reptiles and birds and covers an area of 214 acres.

Most of this information I gleaned from a pamphlet I purchased at the gate. The pamphlet also warned: DO NOT BRING FIREARMS OR WEAPONS OF ANY KIND INTO THE PARK. Possibly, previous visitors had gone hunting or haywire. And successfully, too. For as we wandered around the dry and dusty complex I could not help but notice how a good proportion of the cages and enclosures were empty. No way did the zoo contain 1,600 exhibits, unless insects were included.

'There aren't many animals,' I pointed out to George.

'I have a friend who works here, sir. He will know where all the animals are. Let me see if I can find him.'

I waited by a small cage containing a turkey so scrawny it looked more like a vulture. A sign on the cage read: FOREIGN EXOTIC BIRD.

George returned with a born-again zoo keeper who minutes earlier, since he was covered in grease, had possibly been a car mechanic. 'This is Ram,' George said. 'We were in the army together.'

Ram could speak no English so George became the translator, yet again. How much Ram really said and how much George decided to improvise I have no idea. This was always a problem with George translating.

'Ram says there are not many animals because they die.' George handed me an answer to my original observation.

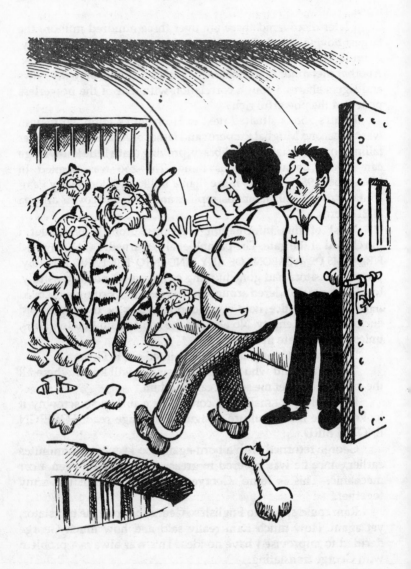

'Die? How?'

Back came the translated reply: 'The water they drink is polluted. The rhino died from gastro . . . gastro . . . '

'Gastroenteritis?' I offered.

'Yes, sir.' He listened to Ram then added: 'Very rare deer died recently after being fed string and polythene and an orangutan died because of the heat.' Ram passed on a few more revelations. 'Also, some animals have been sold or stolen . . . a few have been eaten.'

Ram was happily smiling. It obviously did not concern him that his zoo's contents were vanishing into early graves, trucks and stomaches.

'Where are the tigers?' I asked.

More Hindi, then, 'Ram will take us to their cage,' George replied.

I was getting excited. At last I was about to see a tiger, but when we reached the cage it was empty. I looked around for any suspicious Chinamen.

'No tigers!' George declared and then presumably said the same thing in Hindi. For a moment Ram stopped smiling. He walked off and returned a few minutes later smiling again. George listened to him. 'Sir,all the tigers are having lunch. Ram says for one hundred rupees you can go inside and watch.'

'Go inside?' I had no intention of becoming their second course.

'Perfectly safe,' George said with little conviction, 'but not official.'

We agreed on forty rupees and George willingly volunteered to keep watch outside. Ram pulled back a heavy bolt and we stepped into the dark interior of the tiger house. There were five tigers inside, all adults. Three were white tigers, two were Bengals. Upon seeing us they stopped ravaging their ribs of buffalo and perhaps tried to remember what humans tasted like. Ram picked up a stick and to my horror jabbed one of the tigers. It snarled and lashed out. The bars rattled. They seemed alarmingly insubstantial. It was time to leave. My tiger hunt was over.

Leaving the zoo, shielding my eyes against the heat and dust, I felt something grabbing at my legs. I looked down. It was a beggar, an old man with no legs of his own, just stumps. He moved himself around on an improvised trolley. I gave him twenty rupees and he growled back like an injured animal.

'It's a cruel country,' I said to George as we reached the car.

'It's not cruel to people like you, sir,' he softly replied. 'It's only cruel to people like us.'

When the Road Forks

'When the road forks, take it,' came, one morning, this zen-like fax from my Indian partner. It was his recondite reply and a masterpiece of delegated ambivalence to my suggestion that after producing over eighty campaigns in almost as many weeks—and achieving conspicuously few victories—I ought, perhaps, to be moving on to less combative pastures.

For several months our relationship had been deteriorating and his stares had become either less or more meaningful. It was impossible to tell which. Unquestionably, they had intensified in their duration. In retaliation I abandoned conversation and started staring back. Thus, when together, we stared and when apart we faxed.

Like separated lovers we both blamed each other. I blamed him for not moving the office, as he had so often promised, and releasing me from my twice daily anxiety trip in the lift. I also blamed him for helping me terminally reverse my career into a dusty, Delhi cul-de-sac. In fact, during moments of manic dementia I blamed him for everything from power cuts to Delhi's lack of night life. He, in turn, blamed me for not being able to turn volcanic mountains into abstract molehills, as he succeeded in doing so effortlessly, and for costing him too much money, despite the fact he hadn't paid me for five months. Whoever was more to blame the Indian Rope was turning into a noose.

On reflection it had been a bizarre and frequently frustrating job; like trying to build a house of cards in a gale, and although I had done my best to develop lasting relationships with my clients most had disappeared into the night. Hari Dhoop's embryonic airline never took off, though he did, owing us a considerable sum of money. Nor did Ved ever get back to me on the delicate issue of peddling hooch to Muslims. The coir mattress client who had called me 'doctor' must have found another, less Westernized consultant because I never heard from him again, either. I'm sure Himachal Pradesh is still searching for a long term Director and my attempts to make India's roads safer had ended up in a shredder. On the positive side, however, as far as I know, we are still helping a certain gentleman in Bombay to outlive history, and the temptress has tempted at least a few thousand men to sample her intoxicating wares.

When I informed George I would be leaving at the end of the month he burst into tears. At the time we were driving about as fast as the Premier would go around India Gate. In losing control emotionally he also lost control of the car to an explosion of loud honks.

'George, pull yourself together,' I yelled as a Red Line bus became dangerously intimate.

He dabbed his eyes with the back of his hand. 'What will happen to me?' he asked between sobs.

'You'll get another job, I'm sure.' Angry haired, heavy headed, hypochondriacal, stressed out drivers had to be in short supply.

'But, sir, it takes time to find another job. How will I look after the family in the meantime?'

'I'll give you an extra month's wages,' I promised and he immediately cheered up.

The Big Fish cook also cried on being told I was leaving. It had taken him months but he had finally mastered the art of making scrambled eggs on toast which he tried to serve me at least twice a day.Providing he found an employer who wanted to be egg bound and had a penchant for Indo-Mexican cuisine he would be fine. Even Freddy, the chowkidar, appeared upset over my imminent departure. Only the moonlit mali expressed no emotion, but then the garden was his true employer and the garden was staying.

At work my decision to quit was received with mixed reactions. A few, I suspect, had no idea why I had come there in the first place. Others, no doubt, wished I hadn't—including the Tibetan teaboy who had brewed numerous, toxic spells under the guise of tea and always seemed surprised to fine me alive and comparatively well the following morning. But my creative colleagues appeared genuinely upset if only because their work load would increase dramatically once I left.

'Need you . . . don't go . . . gone,' was Gosh's staccato valediction.

Gautam added more mystically, 'Leave slowly, my friend, and return quickly.'

And Vikki, my part-time secretary, simply said: 'It's been a pleasure being under you.'

It fell upon Krishnan, the office manager, to expedite the necessary and unnecessary paperwork without which India would be a far more arboreal land. The first form I signed caused the phone at Kum Kum to be cut off with unparalleled efficiency.

'I haven't gone yet. I still need the phone,' I protested.

'Can you not use the telephone at the office?'

'No. It never works. Least of all for international calls.'

The thought that he might have to offer another bribe to have the phone reconnected alarmed him. He searched for an alternative option. 'Perhaps you can use a friend's telephone? Send bills to me,' he suggested hopefully.

While my lack of telephone was left on hold we moved on to the juggernaut of Indian bureaucracy: THE INLAND REVENUE. Out of nearly a billion souls less than eight million pay tax in India and I had been a generous member of that elite. Since I was leaving four months into the new tax year I reckoned I was entitled to a rebate. The tax office I visited with Krishnan tempted arrivals with the sign ALL TYPES OF FORMS AVAILABLE FREE. We were already armed with enough forms from the Reserve Bank Of India and the Foreigners' Registration Office to reconstitute a tree. We deposited this load on the crowded desk of a less than cheerful clerk and let time experiment with it's latest barbiturate.

'What he is saying,' Krishnan told me after what felt like months, 'is that you are indeed entitled to a rebate.'

'Good. How much?'

'He says about rupees forty thousand.'

'That will pay for my removal costs. Is he going to issue the cheque now?'

Krishnan blinked at me in amazement. 'Now? Oh, no, no. Not now. In three months, maybe.'

'But I'm leaving next week.'

'It is no problem. I will send you the cheque.'

'I have to tell you, Krishnan, that a rupee cheque outside India isn't worth the paper it's printed on.'

'What to do?' he asked no one in particular.

'Easy,' I came to the rescue. 'Forty thousand rupees is worth about thirteen hundred dollars. I'll write a letter of authorization giving you my rebate and you get the Hong Kong office to issue me a dollar cheque.'

'Hong Kong?'

'Yes.'

'I'll try.'

He didn't

*

There were a number of omens that my time was up. The television had contracted electronic jaundice and was showing everything through a sickly, yellow haze. Five of the six air-conditioners had suddenly blown out thanks to a vicious voltage spike which had also turned the day-glo bile fridge into an oven. During my last weekend the first monsoon of the season uprooted several trees and liberally watered the interior walls. But the final straw was that my stretchy, thumpy music started to squeak as it passed through the cassette player. Stretchy, thumpy, squeaky music. This was one adjective too many.

'What are you going to do with all your things, sir?' George acquistively enquired.

'Some I'm shipping back to England. A lot belongs to the company.' Given his 'love' of music I offered him my unique cassette collection.

'No Jim Reeves,' he said with obvious disappointment after going through the titles.

'Believe me, George, they all sound like Jim Reeves.'

I had set a precedent. He returned later with a present for me. Crudely wrapped in copyright-infringed Donald Duck paper. I opened it to find a gold framed, three foot by two painting of a bright blue Krishna. It was an odd present from a Christian and the last thing I needed to add to my team of luggage. I thanked him as convincingly as I could and he burst into tears again.

'Must you leave, sir,' he pleaded.

'I'm afraid so,' I said.

My own emotions were beginning to turn liquid as I shook each of the staff's hands and then drove out of Kum Kum for the final time. A line of squatters from the jhuggi even waved good-bye.

'I'm going to miss India,' I said to George as we drove south to the airport; despite my head being heavier, my hair thinner, my lungs blacker, the amoebae still opening cafes on the banks of my alimentary canal and my brain still smoking from its display of fireworks. In view of this list I added: 'It's changed me. Forever.'

During my time there Delhi had also changed. Its population had increased by at least half a million and the levels of pollution risen considerably. The city's management was now in the hands of the B.J.P; the nationalistic opposition party who had been directly implicated in the destruction of the Ayodhya mosque. The destruction of Delhi could be their next achievement unless they come to terms with the sheer size and urgency of the undertaking. So far the only evident 'improvements' they've introduced are to make the capital beef-free and increasingly alcohol-free. Given that for many months of the year it's already fun-free, water-free and oxygen-free, they might one day find it's also people-free.

'What will you miss most about India, sir?' asked George as we passed the electronic billboard showing population growth. A film of pollution now covered the numbers rendering them unreadable; a final, contradictory metaphor.

'That's a hard question to answer,' I said. 'My friends, Kum Kum, some of the guys at work, travelling about . . . many things.' Of course, I should have known it was a loaded question.

'Will you miss me, sir?'

'Yes, George. You've been a good driver, and a friend.'

'Then take me to England. Please, sir. I could drive for you there.'

The vision of George driving me down the narrow byways of Devon in a car probably even smaller than the Premier was amusing to imagine. 'If I could, I would. But you know I can't,' I said.

'I wish I had made more of my life,' he sniffed. And I wasn't sure which of us felt sadder.

DEPARTURE

At the airport he fussed over loading my fifteen bags and cases on to a porter's trolley taking special care with his flamboyant gift. Finally, with more tears in his eyes, he gave me an enormous hug which left me breathless. 'God be with you, sir,' were his parting words.

*

When I had arrived in the heat of the night—hungover, jet-lagged and confused—two years earlier I had been more assaulted than welcomed. I had waited so long to pass through Immigration and waited again while the sleepy official methodically checked my six-month visa that in a mad moment of levity I remarked: 'You better hurry up or it will be out of date.' Thereafter his colleagues ganged up on me. When my assorted baggage eventually appeared on the carousel it looked as though it had made its way independently—overland and underwater. Loading up a trolley I staggered through the Green Channel, since I had nothing to declare, and was, as far as I could see, the only passenger stopped. Not only was I stopped, I had to unpack every single bag. As I laid out my life before me a customs man eagerly grabbed my electric toothbrush.

'What's this?' he had asked with a suspicious look on his face. Without its brush attachment it looked like a dildo. I told him its true use. Disappointed he said to his curious colleague: 'Electric teeth.'

But leaving India proved much easier than arriving, even if the check-in clerk insisted I take George's gaudy present on board as hand luggage. With it wedged under my arm I passed through Immigration in a matter of minutes. I was even wished a pleasant flight by the official. A Double Very couldn't have expected better treatment.

Then my luck ran out.

Sitting down in the communal executive lounge I was asked what I would like to drink. I ordered a double gin and tonic.

'Sorry, sir. Only allowed one free drink.'

'What? But that is one drink.'

'Double is two drinks,' I was informed. I had fallen into yet another gin trap.

The time for my flight to depart came and passed. Concerned, I walked over to an airport official and enquired whether the plane to London had been delayed.

'Delayed? Oh, no, sir,' he replied with a grin. 'Just postponed.'

READ MORE IN PENGUIN

In every corner of the world, on every subject under the sun, Penguin represents quality and variety—the very best in publishing today.

For complete information about books available from Penguin—including Puffins, Penguin Classics and Arkana—and how to order them, write to us at the appropriate address below. Please note that for copyright reasons the selection of books varies from country to country.

In India: Please write to *Penguin Books India Pvt. Ltd. 11 Community Centre, Panchsheel Park, New Delhi 110017*

In the United Kingdom: Please write to *Dept JC, Penguin Books Ltd. Bath Road, Harmondsworth, West Drayton, Middlesex, UB7 ODA. UK*

In the United States: Please write to *Penguin USA Inc., 375 Hudson Street, New York, NY 10014*

In Canada: Please write to *Penguin Books Canada Ltd. 10 Alcorn Avenue, Suite 300, Toronto, Ontario M4V 3B2*

In Australia: Please write to *Penguin Books Australia Ltd. 487, Maroondah Highway, Ring Wood, Victoria 3134*

In New Zealand: Please write to *Penguin Books (NZ) Ltd. Private Bag, Takapuna, Auckland 9*

In the Netherlands: Please write to *Penguin Books Netherlands B.V., Keizersgracht 231 NL-1016 DV Amsterdom*

In Germany : Please write to *Penguin Books Deutschland GmbH, Metzlerstrasse 26, 60595 Frankfurt am Main, Germany*

In Spain: Please write to *Penguin Books S.A., Bravo Murillo, 19-1'B, E-28015 Madrid, Spain*

In Italy: Please write to *Penguin Italia s.r.l., Via Felice Casati 20, I-20104 Milano*

In France: Please write to *Penguin France S.A., 17 rue Lejeune, F-31000 Toulouse*

In Japan: Please write to *Penguin Books Japan. Ishikiribashi Building, 2-5-4, Suido, Tokyo 112*

In Greece: Please write to *Penguin Hellas Ltd, dimocritou 3, GR-106 71 Athens*

In South Africa: Please write to *Longman Penguin Books Southern Africa (Pty) Ltd, Private Bag X08, Bertsham 2013*

READ MORE IN PENGUIN